How to Take

10 Years

to Write a Book

(and Rediscover Your Faith Along the Way)

Robert Patterson, Sr.

ISBN 978-1-0980-9227-6 (paperback)
ISBN 978-1-0980-9228-3 (digital)

Christian Faith Publishing, Inc.
832 Park Avenue
Meadville, PA 16335
www.christianfaithpublishing.com

Printed in the United States of America

I would like to thank the following folks, and I dedicate this work to them.

Marian "Momma" or "Nanny" Patterson, for her unconditional love and kindness, plus outstanding cooking and an always-fabulous garden.

Vollie "Daddy" Patterson, for a good work ethic and handyman qualities.

Brothers Kenneth, Keith, and Paul, plus my sister, Julie, for keeping me laughing all the time and not beating me up very often.

My son, Robert Jr, who has grown up to become a heck of a man, husband to Cecilia, and father to Ana.

My dear wife, Paige, whom God sent to me just at the right time in my life.

In-laws Sandra "Mimi" and John "Pawpaw" Measmer, for their acceptance and kindness.

Stepdaughters Abby and Holly, for not treating me like an evil stepfather.

My best friend, Dan Austin, for unwavering friendship across many state lines, hospitality, advice, and use of his motor vehicles.

My friendly and loyal coworkers at Ice Express in Houston, for which I have the pleasure to work with for sixteen-plus years now.

Champion Forest Baptist Church North Klein, for their hospitality, fellowship, and spiritual inspiration.

Sue's daughter, Vicki Jenkins; her hubby, Daniel; son, Kevin, and daughter, Jenna—who calls me grandpa and writes me letters.

Mary and Roger Thompson, for your love and friendship.

And Sue Ann Thompson-Patterson, for putting up with me for fifteen-and-a-half years of love, laughter, companionship, and adventure.

The universe is but specks of dust
blown from God's hand.
                                    —Anonymous

Introduction

In Memoriam Taken Word-for-Word from Sue's Eulogy

Hello, everyone!

I would like to take this opportunity to tell y'all a little bit about Sue. I met Sue while working at Sam's Club in Humble, Texas, in 1998. She was a food-demo lady, and lucky for me, I liked to eat at the demo tables. There could be fifty employees in Sam's (or in Walmart, where she later worked) and she would be the only employee in costume, or at least in a crazy hat appropriate for the holiday—such as rabbit ears for Easter; big Uncle Sam hat for the Fourth of July; or dressing up as a witch, a cat, a scarecrow, or some other costume for Halloween.

Well, we married June 11 of 1999, and from our honeymoon in San Antonio and Corpus Christi on,—we were always looking for a new and exciting place to go. I think the first trip to the Grand Canyon is what really addicted us to traveling, and every year, we methodically planned a new destination.

No place in the United States was off-limits to our shenanigans— Niagara Falls, Hawaii, or Walt Disney World, to name a few.

In 2005, Sue was diagnosed with cancer of the tongue and gums, and after treating it and beating it, she resumed her career in retail.

Then in 2009, she was diagnosed with cancer again; this time on her jawbone. After successful surgery and some radiation, she recovered and resumed her day-to-day routines but with an urgency to get out and experience as much of America as possible while she was still able.

So in 2010, Sue and I decided to sort of retire and take a very long trip which turned out to be 150 days; 13,000 miles; 21 states; most of our money; and memories to last a lifetime. Believe me when I say you know you are compatible with someone when you can spend five months with them in a 250-square-foot living space on wheels.

A side note to this trip: on this trip, a goal of ours was to see a bear in the wild, and we spent nearly a month in Wyoming and Colorado but didn't see one. We saw plenty of what Sue called "fake bears," which were shadows, burnt tree stumps, or odd-shaped boulders. We had to go to a wildlife facility called Bearizona in—you guessed it—Arizona to see actual bears.

Sue was the ultimate packer when going on a trip. She could fit our kitchen, bathroom, a couple of closets, and all my stuff in one piece of luggage. I would get to the hotel room, open my suitcase, and out would come a telescope, a scissor jack, and a couple of cameras; but to her credit, I always had all the stuff I needed.

She liked to collect things, such as brochures from cities, states, and attractions; key chains from many of our destinations, which you can check out over there by the table; T-shirts; hotel shampoo and conditioner; Pepsi merchandise; and no telling what else. There is stuff stashed away in our tiny house that I didn't know existed and haven't discovered yet.

She had a remarkable memory. She knew where anything and everything that we owned was located. I could ask for a purple highlighter that I haven't seen for six years, and she would go straight to it and dig it out for me—that's because she knew I would leave the area a disaster searching for it.

She loved John Wayne and all his movies, and she loved mostly all of the Disney movies—especially the classics. She was very patriotic and would do some little something to celebrate each occasion even if it was simply putting out a little American flag for the day.

She loved going to watch the rodeos, especially the calf roping, chuckwagon races, and bull riding.

She loved cats—specifically her old cat named Oreo that she had, I believe, for twelve or thirteen years. And Sue swore over and over that that cat could say different words like hello or I want, although all I ever heard was meow.

She loved country music when country wasn't cool—like Hank Sr., George Jones, the Statler Bros, Buck Owens and Roy Clark from *Hee Haw*, the Oak Ridge Boys, and others. But she really loved the old-time rock and roll from the '50s and '60s and could dance all night long to those oldies; the '50s-style malt shops were some of her favorite stops.

She rarely drank alcohol, but when she did, it mostly just made her giggle and laugh and ultimately fall fast asleep.

She loved her children and her grandchildren very much and regretted not spending more time with them all.

She loved to ride on our motorcycles and liked to look good while riding! She would get out all the gear even for a short—boots, jacket, goggles, helmet, scarf, do-rag with the flames on it, and sometimes her leather chaps.

Some of her favorite foods were honey BBQ wings, pizza, cheesecake and chocolate cake.

She wasn't afraid to roll up her sleeves and work; and conversely, she wasn't afraid to sleep ten or eleven hours a night.

She loved going on cruises on those gigantic ships. It might have been the exotic destinations and the shore excursions, but I think it was because she liked to eat at those endless buffets. And bless her heart, for she always had to battle motion sickness and seasickness on those trips. You know how she found out about her motion sickness problem? She took a video from our car and the tour bus while at the Grand Canyon, and when she tried to watch the video on our TV, she went running to the bathroom to throw up. Needless to say, she stuck with still photos after that. And, boy, did she take some pictures; we probably have ten thousand on my laptop. But it wasn't all Sue taking the pictures; I'm guilty too. (I point up on the wall)

Did I say she liked to collect things? I've never seen anyone with a fascination for keeping bags—shopping bags, handbags, tote bags, duffle bags, paper bags, assorted grocery bags, and an impressive stash of Walmart bags. I wouldn't say she was a hoarder, but she kept anything that could possibly be of any importance. She was big into keeping receipts and instruction manuals for items we threw away, sold, or replaced ten to fifteen years ago.

She loved Mickey Mouse, Minnie Mouse, Donald Duck, Pluto, and everything at Walt Disney World in Florida. I had to practically drag her away kicking and screaming like a six-year-old every evening after the fireworks.

She liked the Astros and loved going to the games, but I think what she really loved was being close to Brad Ausmus and Craig Biggio.

To sum it up, our sixteen-plus years of marriage was built with love, trust, friendship, compromise, and cooperation but was defined by our adventures. Sue Patterson was kind but tough and courageous. She was a trooper. Early this year, she began her third battle with cancer. Not all of you know this, but a few months ago, I wanted Sue to get to see San Francisco and Yosemite National Park. Although she was in poor shape and miserable much of the time, she let me drag her along to California and we made the best of it, and she managed to have a decent time on what would be our last travel adventure.

Thank you, Sue, I sure miss you.

About Me

As for me, I was the last of five children, born in 1962—which makes me a baby boomer. Although a redhead, which can have its challenges, I had a typical childhood living in modest neighborhoods in Houston, Texas.

I loved to get outside and play with my friends: football, stickball, street hockey, hide-and-seek, tag, climbing trees, building forts, navigating the bayou behind my home, riding bicycles (and a unicycle for a while), swimming, and all the shenanigans associated with my gang of friends.

I made good grades in school, although I sometimes gave less than 100 percent effort—especially as high school was winding down.

I graduated in 1981 from South Houston High School. Partying and ignorance got in the way of me applying myself and going to college. I worked at various jobs and then got married in 1984. And in 1991, I had my son Robert Jr.

We divorced in 1997, and then I married Sue in June of 1999. We went on an extended vacation in 2010. Sue died December 6, 2015 after battling cancer for the third time. In 2016, I met Paige, and we married June of 2017. We currently live in an unincorporated town north of Houston, Texas.

Chapter 1

A Prelude to an Ambitious Lifetime Goal

Day One

So as I sit here reflecting on the day's events, I finally realized right this second that a whole new chapter of my life is beginning right this second. First off, I'm going to have to apologize in advance, for I am not a super detail-oriented person; so the exact timeline may not be accurate.

7:08 a.m.

I woke up for the last time today, Thursday August 16, 2018—not to say it's the last time I'm going to wake up ever, but it will be the last time I get out of bed today, barring being woken up before midnight.

7:15 a.m.

I heat up my water via microwave (one minute and twenty seconds) for instant coffee and pour my plastic cup 3/4 full of dry Raisin Bran. I fixed my instant coffee just the way I like it and proceeded cautiously above the walking, winding body of our male cat (who doesn't seem to mind me kicking him around and stepping on him occasionally by accident) toward the living room then rest comfortably in my old recliner.

At this time, I engage in social media and my favorite online slot game while eating my breakfast and drinking my coffee; kind of the same routine I go through every day whether I have to work or not.

9:15 a.m.

Paige strolls through the living room and greets me with a good-morning kiss, then grabs something to eat out of the kitchen, returns to the living room, plops down in her recliner, and puts on her normal lineup of motivational videos from her motivational-video library on her phone.

10:00 a.m.

I am engaged in the normal worthless playing of my online slot game, social media, and snacking on some sunflower seeds. I note to myself, *Today just might be the one.*

10:45 a.m.

I tell Paige that I could have a better chance at achieving my goals if I had a better laptop computer with the new office software.

11:15 a.m.

I was listening to Rush, still in my wasteful morning routine. I was starting, however, to formulate a plan to get this thing started. I do, after all, have a head start in this adventure, as the ideas, dreams, events that transpired, materials, etc. are already out there like a giant jigsaw puzzle ready for me to piece together with the proper motivation and a little bit of help—which I hope is forthcoming.

12:00 noon

Excitement is building as something deep inside is being stirred up, and my planning of the day events churns on. I check and clear some emails, do another check on social media, check on payments for credit card accounts, get my bonus points for my slot game (super important), and I look for a certain commercial from the '70s or '80s that I believed that Aretha Franklin was in. (She passed away today.) It turns out she was not in the Memorex commercial; that was Ella Fitzgerald.

12:20 p.m.

I finally take off my pajamas and put on some clothes that would be appropriate for both mowing the grass and visiting the Walmart later on.

1:00 p.m.

Paige has to leave for work, and it's time for me to spring into action. I follow Paige through the garage and gas up the lawn mower then mow the front yard (which I do on Thursdays if it's weather-permitting). During this process, I note, *This is really going to happen, isn't it?*

1:25 p.m.

I clean off the lawn mower, do a quick sweep out of the garage, think about checking the mailbox but don't, then start making my way inside the house. I take a pensive look around and then pick up the phone. I go to my email account and start an email to myself.

2:20 p.m.

I send this message to myself…

Day Two

March 3, 2019, 11:52 a.m.

Now I know what the true difficulties of writing a book are: motivation and inspiration.

So much has happened since the last writing! I had the flu (first time in over thirty-five years) and I passed three kidney stones. I thought I was literally going to die. Funny how that process played out: worked hard at my job, straining and exerting as I had not in months; woke up at midnight having what I thought were routine back spasms; experienced the excruciating pain of a stone traveling from my left kidney to my bladder.

If I could experience childbirth, I now know what that feels like. The second one was almost as bad, but the third was less severe. Then one evening at Mom's house, I gently passed a stone while peeing. Of course, I fished it out of the toilet and still have it.

We have made many (necessary) improvements to our house using funds from a refinance loan: foundation, roof, hardwood floor, and bathroom. Side note: Paige was able to begin cosmetology school with a good chunk of the funds.

Most importantly, I have come up with the perfect title for this book!

A decision needed to be made is whether or not to solicit the services of another writer for short story material. I guess later on I will have made a decision.

So other than the obvious challenges of publishing a book—such as money, material, and motivation—there's also having and/or making time for this project. I seem to always be plotting and planning our next vacation(s); therefore, I am resigned to short bursts of energy and inspiration to help make this thing happen.

March 3, 2019, 12:17 p.m.

I'm going to have to place a little of the blame on social media. I spend way too much time on the Facebook. However, I have seen a benefit from it: I have made (and even met) some new and interesting people, plus reconnected with old friends and schoolmates. Also, it has been a canvas of sorts for me to express some thoughts and ideas on a wide variety of topics—including politics. And most importantly, social media is how I met the love of my life, Paige, via a random post and comment!

Monday, April 15, 2019, 6:13 a.m.

Okay, so here I am again trying to get motivated, but it is so difficult with all the problems and distractions that come with a busy life—such as maintenance and upkeep on a house; trying to get out from under our motorcycle loan; finding and completing the purchase of a vehicle for my wife; staying constantly exhausted from such a busy lifestyle, plus the fact that my days off are split up; and often I have to work part of a day or all day on one of my days off!

Some would say that these are excuses, and yes, they are; but in my world, they are legitimate excuses. So here I am once again writing in my spare time, and this time, I am actually driving to work at 5:45 a.m. I don't understand how people can write a book if they are working full time at an ordinary job.

Meanwhile, I spend way too much time and energy messing around on the computer—whether it is "Facebooking," checking email, attending to banking or other affairs, watching highlight videos from the Astros game the day before, or researching and fantasizing about the next travel destination!

I find it interesting that I can only get motivated in short spurts resulting in snippets for the grand finale to come. If I were to recommend a strategy for writing a book, the first thing on the list would be to take notes, take notes, take notes!

Seems like every time I get an epiphany, I'm right in the middle of something or driving somewhere. Going forward, I believe I'm going to have to get a large notepad to keep at my side at all times in case such an epiphany occurs again—which I know it will.

The idea for the title came to me simply by looking at the date which I noticed is quickly closing in on the ten-year anniversary of our trip of a lifetime. So now I must get motivated to set a realistic goal and take the steps necessary to reach my goal and finish my book by May 14, 2020.

Oh, by the way, my motivation for working on this excerpt came from a fortune cookie which said something about achieving your dreams or reaching your goals or something that. Oh look, just passed a billboard that said, "Dare to dream," hahaha.

Monday, April 15, 2019, 6:31 a.m.

Thought: people say that they are a slave to their job or their house or people or a condition, but in reality, we are only a slave to our own actions and behavior.

6:36 a.m.

Another thought: there is a God, and he gives us the tools necessary to get the job done along with throwing both clues and obstacles in our path so that we may make better and better decisions as we get older and older. As far as tools go, I believe I have a decent grasp on the English language and grammar. I even have a halfway-decent vocabulary, which is growing all the time. He also gave us spell-check and autofill just for fun. Well, I've nearly arrived at my job, so ta-ta for now.

4:24 p.m.

Note: God also inspires me with Christian music. He seems to have a way of releasing a song which has meaning in my life at the time of its release. I highly recommend listening to Christian music!

The Gorilla

Wednesday, April 24, 2019, 6:53 a.m.

At this time, I would like to take a break from the abject failures to talk about a success story. Seems my latest motivation has come from the successful deploying of my gorilla mask and subsequent prowling of the Houston Hardy Toll Road. I figure if I can make something as silly as this happen, then I can make anything happen.

So I have sold my latest bags of aluminum cans, and with the windfall proceeds, I purchased a goofy gorilla mask which I don when I'm traveling to and from work on the toll road. I don't know where I got the idea for this; it just came to me one day as a sort of novelty and something for fun along with being a potential motivating factor.

I don't know if it is notoriety I am searching for or a feeling of accomplishment or just good fun. I guess everyone dreams of enjoying at least a little bit of celebrity status.

Wednesday, May 29, 2019, 5:27 p.m.

Here are some early stats for the mask:

Monday, May 27, 2019, (Memorial Day)—wore on the way home in very light traffic; no luck.
May 28—wore to work; one passenger saw me.
May 29—wore home (too dark in morning) and passengers saw and took photos!

Sunday, June 23, 2019, 11:51 a.m.

So one of the difficulties in writing a book is that all the while, life happens, comes, and goes whether you want it to or not. The HTR Gorilla has taken a break. My coworker and dear friend plus motorcycle buddy lies at the VA hospital in MICU, living (if you can say living) out his final days after a tough battle with lung cancer.

Cancer sucks.

Then my wife has just laid to rest her dear grandmother who finally succumbed to Alzheimer's disease.

Alzheimer's disease sucks.

Meanwhile, we have begun attending a new church in the neighborhood, which I like a lot. I just wish I had the courage to ask my new church folks for help with my grief. I left the service (alone as my wife is in North Carolina for Grandma's funeral) and suppressed tears, but when I approached the house, a Chris Tomlin song came on the radio, "My Chains Are Gone," I let out a flood of tears that have long been coming. Man, I needed that!

Now back to my dying friend.

Just got off the phone with the physician who agrees with just keeping him comfortable while continuing to work on some of the outlying symptoms: high calcium, low oxygen, potential blood clots, and other unfavorable complications.

At this point, I don't know if I have the courage to go see him. The last visit was very bad, and with extremely limited communication, all I could ascertain was that he wanted me to take him home to his (hoarded, we found out) apartment. I guess I didn't blame him under the circumstances of having a huge battery of tubes, wires, sensors, hoses, a breathing apparatus, and who knows what else. If it were me, I would want to escape that building too.

Did I mention we have three cats? Well now we have three cats with fleas thanks to me letting them play in the garage. Got a collar on one, but the other two aren't having any of that. Will be interesting to see if we can get the other collars on and administer liquid flea-prevention products. I never knew a ten-pound cat would have the strength of a rhinoceros!

Well guess I'll go mow the lawn and watch a movie, or listen to the Astros on the radio.

Sunday, August 4, 2019, 3:48 p.m.

Nugget I found: "If you are thinking like everyone else, then you are not thinking." (Source: ascendbodymind.com)

Thursday, August 22, 2019, 2:20 p.m.

Life keeps happening. I feel a recurring theme coming on. Maybe I should make a reference to that in the title.

So much going on! If anything, I am finding that the motivation to write comes and goes, often on a whim.

Back to Rick. So Rick—one of my few friends—came in to work a while back and said, "I can't do this anymore." Thus beginning a rapid decline in his health which, in turn, got me nominated to seek power of attorney over his affairs and see to it that his final wishes be carried out.

Turned out that Rick had lung cancer which had begun to spread. Since he had no family in the area (estranged from them for God only knows how long, save a stepdaughter in Nevada), it was up to us coworkers (mostly Ladonna) to ensure he got to the hospital when needed and to tend to basic needs as well as provide emotional support. Tough task.

Late in his demise, the doctors and I agreed that treatment was no longer an option—that Rick be moved to the VA's version of hospice care. Less than twenty-four hours later, my friend passed away. Next came planning and execution of the memorial service, which was frustrating at times.

R.I.P. Ricky, and thanks for donating me your '09 Harley.

So traveling; the one descriptive word which seems to dominate my thinking and define my adulthood. A vacation-planning company offered a deeply discounted cruise, and of course, we accepted. This was only a few months after booking a cruise with our regular cruise line for February 2020.

If there is one thing that really truly excites me, it's planning a trip. I guess I should have been a travel agent.

Meanwhile, the battle continues in the quest to eliminate debt, which sadly is not gaining traction at the present time (go figure) but is still part of our master plan to eventually move to the coast—a new, expensive sliding glass door coming next month after vacation.

My son—Robert Jr.—and his wife, Cecilia, are closer than ever to formally adopting their precious Ana.

Paige bought me a nice secondhand Dobsonian telescope (for Father's Day?) which I have been looking at from across the living room for a couple of months.

Stepdaughter has left early for TCU, resulting in distress for her mother.

I'm going to state the obvious here: it's twenty-five times more difficult to take care of a sticks-and-bricks house than it is to keep up cleaning and maintenance on an RV.

The Hardy Toll Road Gorilla has been in hiatus, but I did come up with an idea to get exposure—a laminated sign with the following verbiage: "Warning, there is a gorilla driving this pickup truck. Take his picture!"

So I will soon tape that to my tailgate on the way home and see what happens. By the way, there have been a variety of reasons for the hiatus: rain, excessive heat, driving a company vehicle, sadness.

I have conjured up yet another scheme for fame and fortune. My idea is a reality show based on a group of friends playing poker and other card games. I have one coworker in the loop and seemingly on board, but this project is going to require some dough-ray-me, time, and effort. See you on TV!

Just got a text this morning from my best friend in Oregon. He had to lay down his motorcycle at twenty-five mph to avoid hitting a couple of four-wheelers. He had road rash, bumps, and bruises, but was otherwise okay. Even after the wreck, he continued in to work!

With the clock continuing to tick away, I had better start accelerating my effort to piece together this body of work along with finding a cheap camera crew for the reality show.

Tuesday, September 3, 2019, 8:56 a.m.

Thought: something that I have discovered on the fly is if you start a project, go all-in on it, commit to it, and execute to its end. Don't start 3,456 projects and not see them to completion. Commit to one and get it done.

Tuesday, September 3, 2019, 9:23 a.m.

There's nothing that I am going to say that you have not heard before, and that's for a reason: all of the cliches, old sayings, age-old advice, et cetera have survived for generation after generation because they are tried-and-true. It's like having the answers to the test: you have to use them when the time comes.

One also must take advantage of opportunities when presented with them and make the most of them.

Back to the title of the book issue. I've decided to go with a multiple-choice format because the choices are all good (and relevant).

Thursday, October 24, 2019, 3:03 p.m.

Unhappiness

So it's been a while since I've written anything. I'm going to attribute this lack of productivity to my seemingly perpetual state of being unhappy. How long have I been unhappy? Who knows—maybe I've always been somewhat dismayed, disappointed, melancholic, negative, etc.—but it seems a lot of the blues began when my best friend and wife of fifteen-plus years passed away.

Really, it could be said that things really went downhill in August 2015, when the third and final cancer diagnosis was given. I'm not a hard or explosive griever; I'm a silent, deep griever. Although the pain of her death was fierce, the sadness was fading, and the personal effects doled out and dwindled down to a few precious items; the underlying sadness does linger and can affect your everyday actions, productivity, and interactions with others.

I also have to add the other factors causing my bad mood: the stress of and people at my place of employment; my lack of a true friend (within driving distance; my current best friend lives in Oregon); my radical lifestyle change (going from living frugally in a travel trailer to the overwhelming responsibility of a three-bedroom home); seeing my stepdaughters much more than my son; not being able to do things that I used to do without feeling rough the next day; not having the means to start up my dream of a nonprofit; not having the drive and motivation to finish *this* body of work.

It was always my intention to write a story about the "big trip" and add to it with short stories, but as time has gone by, I find myself writing about the journey of writing and the struggles along the way!

This is *so* not looking like anything I have ever seen or heard of, and thank goodness! And no, it's not gimmicky; it's my work, my style—like it or not. I believe this will contain one of the longest forewords in history, if not the longest.

Titles. Let's talk about the title. How could I condense the meaning of this work into a short phrase? Too difficult, hence the multiple choice. If I could possibly sum it up, it would boil down to the following: RV story, love story, dreams, the future, and the process.

Thursday, November 21, 2019, 9:10 a.m.

Some tidbits I heard on a montage of motivational speeches:

Overcome the fear of failure.
A person who wants nothing, does nothing.
Just when you think you know it all, you know nothing.

Wednesday, December 18, 2019, 10:09 a.m.

Deep thought: is life simply a series of remarkable and impossible coincidences? I think not.

The Nonprofit

Thursday, January 23, 2020, 3:57 p.m.

Okay, so I was inspired today when a sample (writing) pen came in the mail. The pen has imprinted: "Rolling Signature of America" plus "Spring TX 77389" along with an insignia commemorating six years as a registered entity.

What is this, you ask? This is my brainchild from at least ten years ago, maybe earlier. I have, for many years, wanted to start up a nonprofit organization but have not been aggressive in getting one going. Ideas came and went; but in 2010, while driving around the country, I thought, *How about a travelling charity where folks from all walks of life could see what we have up close and personal, get information about our cause(s), and participate by leaving a permanent mark (literally) on our rolling office!* This is how it works:

1. Buy, beg for, barter for, or by some other legal means, get a new or barely used motorhome. This is the toughest challenge of all, given that motorhomes run in the many thousands of dollars. Ideally, it would be a modest model, straight from the manufacturer without the finished decals or paint on the outside walls.

   [Note: getting an RV manufacturer's owner to donate a new unit will be challenging, to say the least.]

   This would serve as both an office while out on the road and the canvas on which the donors would leave their mark. (I'll explain in a minute.)

2. Acquire all the literature and visual aids regarding the subject charity or charities (books, pamphlets, posters, etc.)

3. Acquire merchandise regarding the charity/nonprofit, for which some would be given out (such as ink pens) and some would be sold as for-profit goods with proceeds going, of course, into the nonprofit coffers.

4. Contact a business that has a large parking lot and can handle an unusual influx of vehicles.

5. Notify the local media of the event, venue, and our intentions.

6. Try to get a law enforcement officer to donate their services for a few hours.

7. People participate and donate.

8. Ultimately, the RV is sold at auction with proceeds going back into the nonprofit (maybe for the next RV, The Signature of America II?).

So you ask, What will happen when people show up?

The Rolling Signature of America will be just what the name implies: a traveling vehicle on which donors to the charity actually sign their name(s) onto the outside of the RV using paint markers. Not sure what would be an appropriate starting amount though. Probably would have to put a grid pattern of some sort on the body of the RV to regulate the size of the signatures. Perhaps the sizes of the signatures would be in proportion to the sizes of the donations?

The vehicle would travel from site-to-site, whether it be daily (not likely), weekends, or on some other schedule or program. Materials pertaining to the nonprofit would be displayed along with the merchandise for sale. A police presence would help keep us secure. Ideally, some local celebrities would attend, give generously, create a buzz locally (and maybe nationally?), plus inspire others to give.

So where are the proceeds going? I'm glad you asked! There are so many worthwhile options such as veterans, stray animals, heart disease centers, a variety of cancers and other diseases centers, hunger, and many others.

What hit home for me was something that struck right here at home: head and neck cancer. Anyone who has come in contact with this cruel disease knows its devastating effects on not only the victims suffering with the disease but also the family members close to the patient. It is my intention to dedicate funds for a scholarship to those students who would be pursuing a career in oncology, specifically in the research and treatment of head and neck cancer. Candidates would have to write up a good synopsis of why they should get the scholarship funds.

Now, me being a fellow who cannot always make up his mind, I have other ideas about where the donations could go. I do a lot of driving in and around the Houston, Texas, metro area; and often see motorists broken down on the shoulder or even in the road. Often all the person needs is some gasoline, a tire changed, a battery, etc.

What if there was a (no-cost) option out there to get folks up and running in a timely manner? Sometimes a tow truck is necessary, but often all the motorist needs is a simple fix. This would also be an expensive charity operationally, as we would need a utility truck, tools and equipment, fuel, plus a mechanic. I would love for a bored retired mechanic to step in and provide this important piece of the puzzle.

Lastly, another topic that has caught my attention is mental illness and varied disorders of behavior. Seems that neurological problems are widespread, perhaps to the degree of being rampant. No one is immune; I've seen occurrences in the young, the old, and everything in between. Monies could be earmarked for scholarships to ambitious students who want to pursue a career in tackling this field of study—whether it be in research, education, or treatments.

What these subjects have done in my world is create the need for many, many more resources as well as more staff to get it all done. Now if I had overwhelming support for this project or successful book sales, I could do a lot of this myself. I have some business skills, some exposure to accounting (although not with nonprofits), and certainly can drive and operate an RV (I have a commercial driver's license); plus I have a network of friends and acquaintances who I believe would help me if asked to do so.

If the resources were available, my dream is for the Signature of America to be a three-headed monster (Cerberus?) and would make creating a logo more challenging. Oh yeah, I need a logo. I tried to create one on my laptop using the paint program, but I am not exactly the artistic type; I'm more of a visionary and a worker bee. Soon I will be reaching out to my Facebook friends for recommendations and advice on logos, and I better start reaching out to RV companies if I ever want to get this thing rolling.

Well, that's what I have to share with you today, got to check on the Cornish game hens in the oven and the load of clothes in the dryer.

Saturday, February 15, 2020, 9:33 a.m.

Note: I'm writing from my desk at work.

So yesterday was Valentine's Day, a day out of the 366 in this year where we celebrate our love for the people in our lives that make us happy. In spite of the somewhat late sending of Valentine's cards, everyone got theirs in a timely manner: Mama, Mom-in-law, wife, Dad-in-law, stepdaughter, and step-granddaughter. Unfortunately, it's also an opportunity to rekindle my grief over losing Sue.

Also, there was a Hardy Toll Road Gorilla sighting after months in hiatus. We had a nice sunshiny day, and I got off work at a reasonable time; and because I waved at a few drivers, I was noticed by two. Sadly, I can drive for miles and miles and miles with my window down, and folks just don't seem to pay attention to other drivers!

During the hiatus, I printed up a sign to put on my tailgate but never could decide how to temporarily affix it to said tailgate. (I didn't trust Velcro to hold in the wind of sixty-five to seventy mph travel.) Also during this time, I checked into an electronic sign that could be put up in the window and taken down on a daily basis, and lo and behold, I found one for about thirty bucks on that large global shopping conglomerate website. After about forty-five minutes of technical heartache and pain, I got the message saved into the system: "There's a gorilla driving this truck! Take pics and post to Facebook."

Also during this past month, I signed up for a back-window advertising company, which unfortunately is taking up just enough of the window space to prevent good vision of the electronic sign. Also interfering with visibility is my large toolbox in the front of the bed. Solution? Remove the toolbox and replace it with a few plastic totes with lids which will also allow the opportunity to organize my tools and other important junk (hope these items aren't stolen). What will probably happen is the little bit of money I will make advertising would be used to replace stolen items.

For a change, I'm in a pretty good mood when writing; so when this work is finished, perhaps some comparisons can be done to see if the content is adversely affected or if there is no change whether I'm mad, glad, or indifferent.

Wednesday, March 4, 2020, 4:15 p.m.

HTR Gorilla Update:

Some days, I'm just not feeling it. However, I feel days ago I was noticed by a couple of other drivers, notably a gentleman in a tractor trailer rig. Then yesterday, I thought I would step up my game by waving a small American flag outside my window but only with limited success.

One lady and a pickup truck saw me and snapped my picture! I'm hopeful that she saw the electronic sign in the back of my window, but I'm not sure. I guess I will have to check the Facebook page. I believe I'm going to have to remove the tint from the portion of the window where the electronic sign shows through, or I will have to mount the sign on the outside of the window which means that I will not be able to use the sign when it is raining.

In other news, I had a very rough couple of days at work over the weekend, then follow that up with a rough dentist appointment. And yes, I voted in the TX primary. Last but not least, we got a replacement cat: a male we call Midnight.

Friday, March 13, 2020, 5:53 p.m.

So I started the day off okay, then got somewhat irritated, then got okay on the ride home. This has been one of those weeks—death in the family, pandemic, full moon, stock market near-crash, and Friday the 13th all in one week! At least I'm alive and have a job (for now, as a significant amount of future business has vaporized due to the pestilence).

My drive home was somewhat fruitful, as maybe five or six motorists saw the HTR Gorilla. This in spite of light traffic; I guess the catalyzer was my frantic waving of my little American flag out the window? No one slowed to take a picture though. Looks like I will have to mount the sign outside the window, or find a way to secure my laminated sign to the tailgate without stripping the paint off of it.

Lost one of my beloved aunts the other day after a long bout with dementia. I really loved her; she used to have quite a sense of humor!

The cats are getting along better these days; much less snarling and fussing and fighting going on in here.

I solicited info from a few publishers, but it seems they all want to talk to me about the book when all I want right now is some rough pricing, guidelines, and procedures for getting published. Am I putting the cart before the horse? I don't think so, but maybe I'm wrong or naive.

In spite of all the travel warnings and difficulties, we purchased an island-hopping Caribbean cruise for next year. Now we have to ponder what to do later this year if anything. Might depend upon if my friend in Oregon comes to town.

Anyway, things are progressing at my pace, and that's fine with me.

Friday, May 15, 2020, 6:43 a.m.

Thought: What separates us from other animals is the ability to improve ourselves.

Saturday, May 16, 2020, 9:55 p.m.

A breakthrough? Perhaps.

So I'm thinking God has intervened—or at least thumped me on my noggin—so I've replied to emails and made a call to a (or the) Christian publisher. Of course, they answered my questions and told me what I have suspected all along: that one needs to bring their work to completion in order to have someone read it, and then they can determine if your work is worthy of being published (by them).

Checking out a few competing publishers will tell you all you need to know about the process, the distribution, and the differences with royalties; the rest comes from common sense and conversing with other authors.

Of course, always lurking in the information packets and in the back of my mind is the realization that the publisher(s) will reject my project.

That brings me back to God. Sitting alone here at home, I could have been adding to the content, but since I lack motivation, I instead turned on the TV to find a movie to watch. I almost settled for a sci-fi monster movie but scrolled on and came upon *I Can Only Imagine*, which I knew was the story of the singer of the Christian band MercyMe and his struggle to forgive his abusive father.

Now I'm not saying there are parallels between this plot and my life, but I can relate to the character's lack of confidence, responsibility, and direction. Although I don't have the singing talent that he has, I have enough of what it takes to bring a compelling story to print.

Still working out the short stories in my imagination soon to be put to paper.

Meanwhile, I sold my pickup, ending my ad campaign for the time being. Replacement vehicle is getting forty-eight to fifty-one mpg.

HTR Gorilla is on hiatus.

We still have incomes, and everyone is fine.

Sunday, May 17, 2020, 10:46 a.m.

Thought: Life throws darts at us, and sometimes God lets one drop off.

Thursday, June 11, 2020, 10:52 a.m.

I can think of a baker's dozen or more of reasons why I *can't* write. Well, here's a good reason *to* write. Today marks the twenty-first anniversary of my and Sue's marriage. I can only imagine how things would be: same old, same old with a few changes.

By now, Sue would be collecting social security. Perhaps she might be working one or two days per week, whatever the law allows. On my end, things would be pretty much status quo: wake up, have a twelve-ounce cup of instant coffee, play slots on my phone, visit Facebook, go to work, come home, contemplate dinner, and dream and scheme on our next vacation trip. The thing is that's kind of how things go now, only with a new cast of characters.

Nowadays, I scheme with Paige and am now more into prepayment than ever before. Our January cruise is almost paid for, except for Wi-Fi and drinks. We are also looking to fly free and visit Sue's daughter in Ohio perhaps in early September.

Speaking of Sue and her daughter, this ongoing pandemic (overhyped or nah?) has provided some time to address the big mess in the garage. I managed to move some stuff around, put some items on shelves, sell a few things, and make decisions about some items that seem to just be taking up space. I tore down an old worktable and put a secondhand shelf set in its place, putting a bunch of my junk on said shelves.

Then I get to some huge plastic totes that came from the old storage room Sue and I used for many years. I probably hadn't looked into those totes in ten or maybe even fifteen years. I open the first tote: wedding artifacts including the guest book, some newspapers, brochures, trinkets, souvenirs, stuffed toys, and a jacket.

The second tote contained books, souvenirs, clothes, magazines, Disney movie videos, old toys, and a huge ashtray built into a large (faux?) cow patty.

Tote number three contained some interesting items: forty-three vintage Pepsi cans, eight vintage Pepsi bottles, one Sprite can, two Coke cans, a US quarters coin-collection book, a Doral cigarette tin container, some old toys (most still in original packaging), and a coin purse that contained some old assorted coins. I'm currently in the process of sorting through the items and putting into three categories: cherished items I want to keep, items to be thrown away, and items to send (or take) to her daughter in Ohio.

Now back to tote one. Among the newspapers were editions referencing the Astros 2005 trip to the World Series; the Rocket's NBA championships of 1994 and 1995; the upcoming millennium; and most notably, a computer-printed copy of a story from a print media outlet covering Brazoria County, Texas. This story chronicled her harrowing moments when a normally fun tubing trip on the Guadeloupe River went terribly wrong. Also included was an account written by Sue herself:

Attention Evangeline Gormley:

It has been six months since the incident, and I still cannot recall of some things that happened with the actual rescue on July 9, 2004. The only thing that is very vivid in my mind is the almost-tragic episode of my adult life.

My husband Robert, my stepson, and my husband's longtime friends went to our annual camping trip, which is to New Braunfels and the river. We rented our campsite at the first crossing. Here we observe the others on the river in tubes and rafts.

Therefore, we made plans to go on the river in our rafts the next day. We decided that one person would drive the others and our equipment to the drop off spot then go back to the camp and pull us to shore. Then do it again with someone else doing the driving until everyone had a chance to raft the river.

While rafting down the river, there were people in tubes enjoying the river. Tim, Ron, and my stepson wanted to go tubing instead of rafting. Robert and I would follow a raft in case someone needed to be picked up after falling off. Once again, there were no incidents.

Now it was my and Robert's turn to tube. Since there were no previous incidents, Tim would start the barbecue and Ron would drive us to the drop off spot. We were having a great time together, floating. I had brought my duck whistle that I got in Branson, Missouri. I had been blowing it at people along the bank as I passed. They laughed and waved at me.

After a while, Robert and I held on to each other, and we're talking. The next thing I know, I was being slammed against a tree in the river and Robert floated along the opposite side of the tree. My raft "climbed" the tree, which in turn threw me off the tube.

With one hand, I held on to the tree and wrapped my legs around a submerged limb. Not for long, the limb broke, and I screamed. I had been screaming for help. "Robert!"

I also called out that I was not kidding and that I really needed help, in hopes that this statement would get someone to at least look for the sounds. I kept going under the top of the water. Each time I felt a rock under my feet, I tried to stand up but was knocked off by the current. Each time I came above the surface of the water, I yelled.

At some point, a voice from my swimming class that I took at San Jacinto College North Campus came into my head, *Float! Try to float!* So I did but couldn't. Tried again and again to float. This floating on my back saved a little energy, plus allowed me to get some needed air. I could not stay floating very long. The waves would put me back under.

I was running out of time. I knew it. I kept up the yelling. It seemed like my getting back to the surface was getting more difficult every second. Then out of the surface came, "Grab my hand!" So I made my way to the surface again. Someone grabbed my hand and arm, pulled me up, hooked my arm around a tube, and said, "Don't let go!"

At that point, I said, "OK" or "Yes, sir" or something to that effect. He was paddling me back to the shore where a man, a woman, and Robert told me to sit on the bank. I sat, doubled over.

Whenever I sat up straight, water gushed out of my mouth. They people told me to let it out because it was coming from my lungs. I had noticed my left leg hurting whenever I was being brought into shore. It was black-and-blue and swelling up fast. I don't know too much more at this point. All I knew at that time, was that I had been rescued from drowning by a man on a tube, and people were helping me on shore.

Ron had come looking for us because we should have been back at camp by now. He saw us and stopped his pickup truck by the road. I was being carried to his truck by the man onshore. I got in the truck and was taken back to camp. It was difficult to walk on that leg for a few days, but it's OK now.

I do not know the names of all the people that helped me. I did get a call from Christy Loftus of Brazosport College—the facts.com— who said the man on the tube was Stephen Husky, a lifeguard from Lake Jackson. Russell Carter and Keith Loeffler also swam out to me. There are not enough words in the English language to express my gratitude and thanks for this heroic rescue.

There were many people on and beside the river that day. Why these people chose to help a complete stranger in need can only be described as an act of human kindness and heroism.

Sunday, April 19, 2020, 9:39 a.m.

After the last entry, I was thinking I shouldn't submit thoughts going forward unless I had something compelling or significant to say to avoid being redundant. To only report on my progress. To share with you the amazing forward leaps in the process. However, with the continued coronavirus emergency, I felt compelled to write.

While many are out of work, my employer is still operating, albeit at about ten percent of normal sales for this time of year due to the closures and scaling down of local restaurants along with the postponements and cancellations of all special events. This creates a unique situation where we are staying open for business but operating at a huge loss, which is not sustainable for long.

My wife is not working as the salons were shut down at the onset of the crisis, but she is receiving cash benefits above and beyond her normal pay. What this pandemic event has done is put a wet blanket of stress on the shoulders of every American. Now the good news is as I write this, the country is on the verge of reopening businesses and restarting the economy. The schools will remain closed to the end of the school year though.

Meanwhile, we closed on refinancing the house, taking advantage of the lowest interest rates available. This move allowed us to pay off a vehicle and inject some cash into our bank account which will go toward paying down some credit card debt and enhancing our trip coming up in January next year, along with ensuring we have some cash for emergencies.

Although we as a married couple are not great with finances and budgeting, we did do something about it a few years ago: we attended Dave Ramsay's Financial Peace University at our (former) church! I highly recommend this program for anyone wanting to ensure themselves a secure financial future. All ages, creeds, colors, backgrounds are welcome. In case you're wondering, no, we're not drastically altering our lifestyle (although we should for the best results); but we are much more aware of where our money goes and where future money will be allocated.

The gorilla has frequently been seen riding the toll road, which has been toll-free during this crisis. The problem is traffic is much lighter and faster than normal, so the opportunities are much fewer. On average, about two or three people see me and wave. I even installed my sign on the outside of the back window, but it doesn't seem to be getting noticed.

In other news, a litter of kittens magically appeared in our back-yard a few days ago, giving my wife another project (feeding them and finding homes for them) to go along with her other ones: sand and paint a rescued nightstand, remove and replace the bathroom medicine cabinets (me doing the work), plus continuing with her cosmetology schoolwork. (She's close to completion and testing for her license.)

Boss is giving us all an extra day off per week in order to lessen the chances of exposure within the workplace; and one would think I would take advantage of the time by working on this book, but I'm finding it hard to get inspired. I guess the underlying tension and uncertainty of the situation is to blame? Or is this just a lame excuse? Oh well, life goes on and I still have stuff to do around the house, and I am eating the elephant one bite at a time.

Every time I think about it, I question the title of this book, so I'm going to offer some alternate choices on the cover.

Now that we have some extra money, I need to decide whether to pay upfront for publishing or have the publisher take a portion of the sales for the publishing fee.

Also, always on the back burner is the nonprofit, which will require filing with the IRS—with a hefty filing fee of course.

Still no memorial service for my aunt until restrictions are lifted.

By the time of my next entry, I will have completed the short stories which will be injected into the body of the travel blog, and I will have reached out to the publishers.

Wednesday, October 14, 2020, 7:23 p.m.

It so happens that I'm a procrastinator. Always have been, always will be. It's how I'm hardwired. All throughout school, I tended to wait until the last day, hour, even minute when getting assignments done. Forty-page research paper? No problem! Wednesday night at 11:30 p.m. is a great time to get it done. Paper-mache art project? No problem, 10 p.m. Sunday night it is. Calculus homework? No problem, I'll get right on that thirty minutes before school starts. So you see what my pattern of behavior is, and this project is no exception. Again, it comes down to motivation, making the time, and "feeling it."

One major issue I've experienced is that most of my quality thoughts come when I'm alone in my car, usually on my way to work. I'm definitely a morning person, up at 4:30 to 5:00—usually no later than 6 a.m. regardless of my work schedule. Driving down the freeway at sixty-five mph is not ideal for taking notes, but when I come up with something profound to say, I'll find a way to jot it down.

Lots has happened since my last entry: Mom had a bad fall and had to be taken to the hospital. After a week or so, they let her go home, but she was bruised, sore, and sporting some cracked vertebrae. Normally an active person, she has had to take it easy and use a walker. Mom is the matriarch of the Patterson family, and I owe a debt of gratitude for the manners, discipline, cooking skills, and many other traits inherited from her DNA. Yesterday she celebrated her eighty-sixth birthday!

Recently, I sold Rick's Harley; it just wasn't me. I prefer a much larger bike, and since I rarely rode the Sportster, it made sense to get rid of it. Of course, there's more. Occasionally I look at listings on the Facebook marketplace, and one morning, I saw something that I had to have: a bus. Yes, a freaking big, long bus. The price was right, and after we saw it in person, we decided to buy it with the intent to convert it to a recreational vehicle.

I haven't spent much time on the subject of religion, but it bears mention as it has leapt to the forefront of my life. As a young child, I remember our family going to church every Sunday and possibly some Wednesdays as well. Rowe Lane Baptist Church in the South Houston area. I remember liking Sunday school but not the main service. I think it was intimidating to me, and I was very young.

I don't know when, but we stopped going to church, and we moved to a new area of town. My best friend at the time (Gary) was in a Catholic family. He invited me once to go with them, but that wasn't my cup of tea.

Fast-forward to my teens when I met some new friends who happened to go to church. I started going to South Shaver Baptist, but I'll admit it was mostly for the fellowship and playing organized basketball. I even went to Summer Camp and enjoyed it.

Side note: I was beginning to get into things I shouldn't—such as cigarettes, drinking and cursing excessively, and I even snuck a pack of smokes into my luggage at camp. Well, as high school wore on and I embraced my increasing independence, I drifted away from the church.

That was early '80's. Every so often, I would find my way into a church led by someone else's action. I believe I made it into a Pentecostal and a Methodist church for Easter and Christmas services.

Now fast-forward to 2016, a few months after Sue's passing. Me being one to quickly get over bad happenings, combined with a need for companionship, led me to put myself back into society as a single man. That's when I met a woman at a Facebook friends gathering, and we hit it off. Unfortunately, the main thing we had in common was losing a spouse, and after a few weeks, we broke up and went our separate ways.

Now toward the end of this relationship, something magical happened. One day I posted (on Facebook) that I couldn't decide what to have for lunch and was having to settle for a (room temperature) can of mixed vegetables and had a picture to prove it.

Here's where God intervened and led me to Paige, who I didn't know existed until she commented on my post that she hated to see me eating that and would cook me something if I needed. Next thing you know, I'm checking out her page and profile, and then asking her out to a dinner date. One thing led to another, and here we are married for three-plus years.

Paige was going to a Lutheran church with her two daughters every Sunday, and I decided to join them. I enjoyed the music and the message but wasn't used to their doctrine. So now I need to revisit my friend Rick and his memorial service which was at a Baptist church. Turns out that Champion Forest Baptist was moving one of the campuses to a new location and new building, and not far from our house. Since I enjoyed the memorial message from Pastor Trammell, I wanted to attend services at the new location. We loved the church and the warm welcome we received and have been attending regularly ever since, be it in person or online.

Now back to God. If anybody knows me and how I think, you would be skeptical about my newly found/newly embraced religious beliefs. I've always been cynical, practical, questioning, and skeptical about a lot of things—including God and the Bible. Having an inquisitive and scientific mind has always kept me from fully understanding and, frankly, buying what they (the churches) were selling. I'm sure this is the case with a lot of folks as people tend to be skeptical when it comes to things they cannot see or understand. Sometimes things just happen and can only be chalked up to divine intervention:

1. Probably August of 2016, I had an event to set up at a barbecue cookoff early one Saturday morning at the University of Houston main campus. What I was doing was setting up three large drinking water tanks (with six spigots) and filling with ice and water (from a couple of 230-gallon water totes using an electric pump) and getting out before all the contestants started arriving.

About halfway up to 120 gallons, one of the spigots failed and was gushing water to the ground. Meanwhile, a gentleman had showed up and was working in and around his booth area. Upon hearing my distress signal (cursing), he said, "Hold up, I think I got something for it."

Maybe a half a minute later, here he comes with a new spigot in the package and hands it to me. I quickly got it out, pulled the old spigot out, and replaced it, thinking, *Wow, that was a miracle!* However, there was more work to do, and I was falling behind. I remember thinking if I had a forklift, I could speed the process of filling up by lifting the water tote above the tank and opening the big fat valve on the bottom.

Looking across the lot, I saw a forklift parked by the porta cans. I was hoping there would be a key. Walking up, I saw there was no key. But wait, this is a Toyota lift, and I have a key—and yes, it fit; and yes, I got on and masterfully finished the task at hand.

2. and 3. Recently on a Tuesday morning, while I'm roaming the lot at my work facility, I noticed a coworker moving a half-filled water tote around with the forklift. I walked up to him and asked where he was going with it. He said they were cleaning up the warehouse, and he was going to dump the water into the storm drain.

I said, "Are you sure we want to do that? I went through a big hassle to get that water from retail (our other location) the last time the water was off."

He said, "Yeah, boss wants to clean it up."

So I walked away and went inside the office to my desk. There I proceeded to look at a stack of mail which was five identical envelopes from the DMV. I pulled each one from its envelope, laid them down, and began looking for the renewal notices so I could identify the truck or trailer involved. (I marked the renewal with the asset number.)

I found them and started matching sheets. First one matches the first sheet. Second one matches the second sheet. Third matches the third; fourth with the fourth; and, of course, the last one was a match. I don't know the odds of that happening, but it must be huge.

I mentioned what happened to a couple of guys in the office, and they were somewhat amazed. Okay, so I needed to go to the restroom, and when it came time to wash my hands—well, of course there was no water! Upon investigation, I found out a crew was putting in a hydrant a couple of blocks over.

These kinds of small miracles probably happen all the time, but we aren't aware or maybe aren't paying attention. Do these things happen in your world? I bet they do. Needless to say, my faith is stronger each day, and yes, I still listen to KSBJ Christian music radio.

Another subject I want to touch on is our vacation plans. We went from an island-hopping cruise (cruise cancelled) to a week in Trinidad and Tobago (no international visitors) to a week in Costa Maya, Mexico. Maybe I will finally get to go parasailing. After shifting gears a lot and moving money around, we also booked a Caribbean cruise for 2021 in autumn. We are looking forward to the January trip if it happens; God willing.

Lastly, I need to say sayonara to the gorilla. It's only now, at the end, that I understand what the HTR Gorilla represents: just another excuse to delay completion of this body of work. Although I might use the mask as a prop or something else practical, I shall no longer use it as a crutch for a leg that isn't broken!

The excerpts that follow are the actual day by day account of before and during *a trip of a lifetime*.

Life throws darts at us, and sometimes God lets one drop off.

Chapter 2

A Circle of Life

Sixty days to go.

Well with two months to go before my wife—Sue—and I take off in our motorhome to see the good old U.S.A. There is much work still to be done. I have to finish tweaking the RV to get it ready for the road, including registration/inspection, preventive maintenance, a couple of tires, etc.

Meanwhile, you should see the inside of our house: it looks like a mini-storage facility! Sue has given her employer notice of intent to retire, and I will follow suit soon. It's much more difficult for me to leave my job than for Sue, as I really like what I've been doing—and the money is decent too. This is the first of many posts which will chronicle our progress in this incredible adventure.

March 30, 2010 at 6:28 a.m.

Okay, now hello again.

Forty-seven days to go. We will accelerate into full prep mode soon. RV has been serviced: generator was removed, state-inspected. I have given notice to my bosses, and while they are devastated to see me leave, on the other hand, they are happy for me that our travel dreams are going to be fulfilled.

We are beginning to put certain items up for sale and spreading the word about some big-ticket items we will be parting with.

Circa April 30, we will start aggressively selling ninety percent of our household items; Greensheet ads forthcoming.

Today I will be working on a thorough cleaning in the RV and retrofitting the genny compartment for a series of six-volt batteries which should give us an extra four hundred amp-hours of reserve power. Once the unit is cleaned, we will start placing some key items inside as that will begin to give us an idea of the practical capacity inside our future home.

April 4, 2010, at 5:33 a.m.

Greetings!

Forty-two days to go…

Now that I have cleaned out the RV and installed the battery bank, I will be looking at the loading of some supplies and other items that are must-have to get an idea of what we can take and what has to go. As one can imagine, it's a daunting task to shrink a three-bedroom plus garage house down to a thirty-two-foot house on wheels with a trailer.

April 10, 2010, at 11:29 a.m.

Hello again!

Thirty-five days to go.

Having trouble with the hot water heater, so we will have to fix or take cold showers! All other systems are functioning properly, including my 420-amp hour battery bank. I will need to install the two small solar panels either on the roof or on some sort of board/platform that is portable. The big sell-off is starting now, but the big bang will be toward the end of April. I'm looking for a used trailer; however, a new one isn't out of the question. The landlord has been notified; I still have many utilities and such to deal with.

April 17, 2010, at 10:58 a.m.

Well now looks like twenty-eight days to go! Finally, all systems are a hundred percent thanks to Rick who helped fix the hot water heater (loose wire). Yesterday I arranged for the gas, water, electric, cable, and cell phones to be cut off. We will be getting a pay-as-you-go phone to cut costs.

Next weekend we will be starting up the yard sales; we got lots of stuff to sell! Although my bosses know I'm leaving, my coworkers still do not. Guess that news is coming soon.

My friends Tim and Scott Sizemore are talking about a going-away party. (Yahoo!)

April 24, 2010

Wow! It's hard to believe, but we're only twenty-one days from leaving! We are now in full-blown get-ready-to-go-mode. We have a lot of work to do, especially selling off our unnecessary stuff. I can tell you it's really tough to work on a project when you are still working full-time on your real job.

April 27, 2020

Hello, all!

It's Tuesday, April 27, and the days are seemingly racing by. Sue had a mini yard sale on Sunday and sold a few items—only a thousand or so left! I sent out an email to some family and friends with the heads-up and first pick of the big-ticket items.

If it's weather-permitting on Saturday, Sue will put on a bigger yard sale with signage and such. I went to Dairy Queen, hooked up to Wi-Fi and loaded all my websites into favorites, went to an eye doctor to update my glasses. (I found out I have the very, very beginning of cataracts.)

We packed a *ton* of stuff into the RV with a lot more to go. Sue has three more days at Walmart. (She's at the end of her rope and can barely muster the energy to go the last days.) Now I'm looking into getting one of those prepaid phones, probably from Verizon; they have a $100 per year deal. I need to rent a storage soon for my son's things and find somewhere to park his car for a few weeks.

Sunday, May 16, 2010

Hello!

This is the day we have been waiting for! After an endless amount of hard work—including packing, yard sales, planning, last days at my former job, and saying goodbyes to friends and family— we are taking off today, Sunday, May 16, around 2:45 p.m. We're leaving so late in the day because we have to clean up the house and meet the landlord to secure our deposit. We have a free hotel night at Isle of Capri Casino Hotel Lake Charles, so we won't have to rough it just yet. Tomorrow we will get to Biloxi, Mississippi, to stay a couple of nights.

A written record of an epic journey.

May 25, 2010

Sorry for the gap in communication; I have had difficulty getting Wi-Fi and making it work! We spent a few days navigating the Natchez Trace Parkway, staying a few nights in state parks and some in various parking lots in Mississippi. Not really anything notable to mention, mostly fresh air and wooded scenery and an occasional river or stream.

Now we are in our fourth day around the Great Smoky Mountains National Park. Sue and I have been staying in and around Pigeon Forge, Tennessee. No large parking lot is off-limits! This place reminds me of Branson, Missouri. There is much to do and see, but the coup de grace is definitely the Smokies! It's a must-see and a must-ride on a motorcycle.

Today we're heading through Knoxville into Kentucky, where we hope to spend a few days in some remote locations.

Happy holiday-weekend to everyone; I hope to give more regular updates.

Scott, your brother is the one who brought up the idea of a going-away party, but we got *really busy* there at the end before we left and didn't hear from Tim and Sam again. Y'all be good. We'll see you hopefully in November.

Your friend,
Rob (Dr. Duke)

May 29, 2010

Greetings from Leesburg, Ohio!

Although I have to report, we almost didn't make it here or anywhere! Yesterday (Friday), we were at Kincade State Park in Northern Kentucky. Sue was coming back from an ice cream run on her scooter when a wicked thunderstorm blew up quickly (a microburst) only lasting a minute or two, but it knocked over a bunch of trees—including one onto our motorhome and trailer!

We were standing outside in the storm's chaos, trying to park and cover-up the scooter when the tree fell over onto the top of the RV. Fortunately we weren't hurt at all, but our house-on-wheels got beat up on top: a gaping hole in the roof and a broken AC cover. Also damaged was the right-side mirror on the Honda.

Thanks to the quick-and-organized response of the county emergency people, the tree was removed from atop our house and other trees from the road, and one other from some tenter's canopy. They removed our tree so fast that we didn't make the video for the news the next morning; they did show the drunk guy's camp, which wasn't even affected by the storm.

Thanks a million to Vicki's hubby, Daniel, who helped me make the repairs today using some items he had around his home (plus my duct tape). Looks like after a few days here we will take off westward toward Indiana, Illinois, and Wisconsin.

Thanks to *all* our friends who want to keep up with our travels! I promise to try to do a better job of blogging and Facebooking; it's just difficult getting a free internet connection (McDonald's, Starbucks, Dairy Queen, etc.) We will put up some pics soon.

Ta-ta for now,
Dr Duke
Leesburg, Ohio (east-northeast of Cincinnati)

Saturday, August 18, 2010

It's been a while, so I'll hit the highlights.

After a short stay at the Jenkin's home in Leesburg—in which we mostly visited with the family—we headed out toward Dayton to pick up the I-70 through Indiana. We only stayed one night at a free campground (horse trailer camp) with no electric or water.

Heading west down the I-74, we were in need of water for our fresh H2O tank but couldn't find any connection compatible with ours, and we didn't want to pay for one. Luckily, we went across the road from a Pilot truck stop to a local restaurant where we noticed a *very long hose* around the back of the building, hooked up and ready; that's where our current supply of water came from (pirated water).

The next day, we traveled a few miles to a little town called Pontiac (named for an Indian warrior) which had an awesome Route 66 museum along with an adjacent war museum—all of which were free! Then we left Pontiac and headed toward Chicago, stopping about thirty miles from the city at a Cracker Barrel (where I'm typing this message) which happily is right next to a hotel which is providing free Wi-Fi for our surfing pleasure.

Saturday, weather-permitting, we have some destinations planned in Chicago before we resume our travels westward.

June 9, 2010

Greetings from Hudson, Wisconsin right at the western border of Wisconsin and Minnesota. Despite some rain, we explored Chicago on the Honda and tried to get to US Cellular Field but was not situated where we could get to it, so we saw Soldier Field instead.

When we arrived at Sears Tower, it began to rain hard; so given the poor visibility, we didn't go up the Tower but took pics from the grounds. Then it was over to Wrigley Field (it stopped raining), and the park is charming as well as amazing given its age. Then it was time to pack up and head toward Wisconsin, stopping in Beloit for restocking. We saw a lot of those wind farms up close along the way.

Next day, it was off to Wisconsin Dells, Wisconsin—a scenic river and resort town with much to offer the tourist. Wisconsin Dells *is the waterpark capital of the world!* From Noah's Ark (the largest) to Mount Olympus, they got a park for everyone.

We boarded a tour boat and cruised the Upper Dells, a particularly scenic geographical locale carved out by glaciers. Next day, we walked the 1/4-mile river walk and through downtown to see the markets and attractions and bought our souvenir Wisconsin cheese.

For lunch, it was Dave's BBQ (very good), then we went in the cheesy haunted ghost mansion ($5 each) before boarding the second half of the boat tour on the Lower Dells. Not quite as good as upper but still a nice stretch of the Wisconsin River!

After taking more pics of downtown, we called it a day and went back to camp.

The next day, it rained, so we broke camp and headed out toward Saint Paul, Minnesota. As the motor home started to run poorly, we stopped for the day at Walmart in Eau Claire, Wisconsin.

Cheers,
Dr Duke

Monday, June 14, 2010

Hello, this time from Happy Holiday RV Resort near Rapid City, South Dakota!

From Eau Claire, Wisconsin, we did a lot of driving and headed to Saint Paul. Our "house" wasn't running very well, so we had it looked at in Minneapolis; it needed a fuel filter and carb adjustment, and we went ahead and got the oil/filter done as well. Wow, over three thousand miles already!

We found a good place to park close to the Mall of America (people come from all over the world to visit) and walked over to see what the hype was about. Wow, the place is huge—five floors and a gigantic amusement park smack-dab in the middle of it all. We had some really good Thai fast-food before calling it a night. We must've walked five miles! We watched the Blackhawks win the Cup too.

I asked Sue about the tick.

Sue was complaining that her ear was itching—that there might be something stuck in there. Upon close examination, I found a brown tick in her ear and pulled it out with tweezers! She didn't seem as horrified as I thought she would be, which was typical of her behavior.

Next we took the I-35 south to get on the I-90. Along the way, we stopped at the Village of Yesteryear in Owatonna, a collection of buildings from the late 1800s to the early 1900s. Since the only tour was at 1:30 p.m. daily and the time was 3:15 p.m., we could only look at everything from the outside and peek in through the windows.

The weather has not been kind to us lately—lots of wind, cold, and rain. Anyway, next we stopped off at Blue Earth, a small town which just happens to have a fifty-five-foot statue of the Jolly Green Giant (and a little gift shop).

While we were taking pix of the JGG, a local AM radio personality scooped us up for an interview to be aired on Monday the 14th; the weekly show showcased travelers who stopped to look at the statue.

That evening, we stayed at a highway rest area which has a memorial to the completion of the I-90. After yet another "thunderstormy" night, we started our day (our eleventh wedding anniversary) traveling west to Sioux Falls, South Dakota. We were surprised to find actual falls; they were impressive, and the city park was huge and included informative plaques, historical buildings, and an observation tower.

From Sioux Falls, we headed west toward Rapid City, stopping in Mitchell. We stayed the night in Cabela's parking lot and had anniversary dinner at Whiskey Creek restaurant. When we got back to the "house," we noticed a guy out in the lot had a *bald eagle* on a leash; we got to get about ten feet from the amazing bird! It turns out this guy was with an eagle preservation society, so it was legal.

Saturday, we headed west, still windy/rainy, stopping off at the rest area near Chamberlain for a few minutes. We ended up staying for an hour to look at an impressive display of the journey of Lewis & Clark. Next we crossed the mighty Missouri River and stopped in Kadoka for the 1880s western town which had plenty of roadway signs preceding it. We thought it would be cheesy, but it turned out to be pretty good old west nostalgia. We stayed overnight at an overflow truck parking lot, listening to the rain once again.

Not discouraged, we set out the next morning to Badlands National Park. We drove the 240 loop; it was an *amazing* thirty-five miles of scenery: cliffs, gorges, canyons, spires, buttes, and colors. Never knew what a special place the Badlands is!

From there we followed the thousands of signs (they started three hundred to four hundred miles back) to the Wall Drugstore in Wall, South Dakota. Again, we weren't expecting much but were pleasantly surprised. And we weren't the only travelers lured in; there seemed to be a thousand people in the huge complex which encompassed a full city block on both sides of the street. Drugstores, souvenir shops, novelties, cafes, clothing, and other specialty shops, plus lots of kid-friendly stuff, photos, and western decor.

After that, we continued to Rapid City where we did laundry and stayed the night at—you guessed it—Walmart.

Friday, June 18, 2010

Greetings from Montana!

Rain has let up for several days now, giving us the chance to see a lot of stuff more comfortably. From the Happy Holidays RV Park, we set out on the motorcycle toward Mount Rushmore. Along the way, we stopped and rode a tram up the side of a mountain and got our first good view of the presidents. Coming down was a lot of fun on an alpine sled going at speeds up to forty mph!

Next we drove to Mount Rushmore National Park and took pictures from up close. Then it was off to the Crazy Horse Memorial—a work in progress but still amazing (it will be the largest memorial in the world if they ever complete it). The facility had a large museum/cultural exhibit and a movie—really neat stuff. Perhaps we could come back in twenty to thirty years to see the progress.

From there we entered Custer State Park and got on the Wildlife Loop, where we saw many deer, antelope, prairie dogs, and buffalo—one of which took up residence on a median at a highway intersection! Upon leaving Custer State Park, we took the long way around back to camp and called it a day.

The next day, we left Rapid City (which, by the way, has life-size statues of all the presidents at every corner in one section of downtown) and headed to Sturgis, drove through town, and took some pics. With no rally going on, it wasn't exactly noteworthy.

Then we headed south to Deadwood, South Dakota. It turned out to be a cool little town, and we took an hour tour bus, seeing most the town—including the cemetery containing Wild Bill Hickok and Calamity Jane! A very informative tour. We got off the bus and stepped into the Saloon No. 10, where they had a reenactment of the assassination of Wild Bill; then went outside to catch the 4 p.m. reenactment of an old west shoot-out (a poker game gone bad).

Next we made our way throughout the various old buildings (all of which had a working casino), including the Adams Museum. We then left Deadwood, got back on the I-90, and drove to Spearfish, South Dakota where we parked on a secluded backstreet very near a Walmart. Storms in the area had us a little nervous that night.

The next day, we were awakened early by what sounded like a siren of some sort—still don't know if it was a tornado warning siren or what! We survived that and headed west into Wyoming, got on the 14, then the 24 to Devil's Tower National Monument. Wow, it's really killer up close, and the view getting over to the tower was spectacular!

From there we started heading for any large city we could find, as our toilet was malfunctioning and needed replacing (especially after I got to working on it). We tried Gillette and Buffalo before hitting pay dirt in Sheridan, Wyoming. Of course, we found the Walmart, and I quickly installed the new can, then we had Chinese buffet and called it a night.

On Friday, a nice sunshiny morning (this morning), we headed toward Billings, Montana, and stopped at the Little Bighorn Battlefield National Memorial outside of Hardin, Montana. We walked the grounds and attended a narration of the events before and during the battle at which Major General George Custer and all his men lost their lives; this story was told by a Crow nation native park ranger.

This large area of Montana is within the Crow reservation. We saw many gravesites, monuments, and artifacts.

From there we continued on to Billings, Montana, to the McDonald's where I'm writing this update. From here we haven't a hundred percent decided if we will go to Yellowstone or west, all the way to Seattle and then come back to Wyoming. Decisions, decisions.

Friday, June 25, 2010

Well, we decided to take advantage of the good weather and go into Yellowstone National Park through the northern entrance at Gardiner, Montana. There were many free campgrounds along the way on the U.S. 89; but about half of the campgrounds in the park were full, so we picked the first one—Indian Springs. We then set out on the moto about 3:00 p.m. and did the upper loop—seventy-five miles—and saw beautiful scenery and the Norris Geyser Basin with its many steam pots, hot springs, steamboat geyser, and much more.

The route took us high into the mountains above the snow line. (It was cold up there.) We saw Tower Falls and Mammoth Hot Springs and many deer, antelope, buffalo, and a black bear from a distance. (The bear caused a 1/4-mile backup on the road.) We were rained on occasionally but were dressed for it.

The next day, we took off at 10:00 a.m. to do the lower loop. We saw the lower and midway geyser basins, then over to Old Faithful.

We arrived there at 1:00 p.m. and expected eruption at 1:34 p.m. What do you know; it happened on time, really cool!

Next it was up the mountain, across the continental divide, and through Craig Pass at 8,262 feet. That took us to West Thumb Geyser Basin, then alongside breathtaking Yellowstone Lake. We bypassed Fishing Bridge and Bridge Bay and went on to see Mud Volcano and Sulphur Cauldron. Next it was Canyon Village with the really cool upper and lower falls on the Yellowstone River; and then what's known as the Grand Canyon of Yellowstone. (They ain't kiddin'. It's amazing.) After fueling up, we drove back to camp in the rain, close to nightfall.

Monday a.m., we broke camp, gassed up, and headed east on the 212 toward Cody, Wyoming. More spectacular scenery on the way and through a nice little town called Silver Gate. The next stretch of 296/120 was an up-and-down, incredibly scenic route that included rapids, huge canyons, waterfalls, and a killer ride up to Dead Indian Pass (eight thousand feet), which was some of the most beautiful high elevation scenery you'll ever see!

After some minor engine and brake overheating, we got into Cody, did our laundry, then parked for the night at Walmart. While there, we discovered Cody has city-wide Wi-Fi!

Sunday, June 27, 2010

Okay, friends.

While in Cody, we went on the scooter to the Tecumseh Trading Post Miniature Village and Museum (free) where there were many stuffed wild animals and horns on exhibit and the town of Cody from the 1800s in miniature with working train and audio. Museums have many artifacts and info.

Next, onto Old Trail Town, where the past is preserved (old buildings, fixtures, artifacts.) Then six miles down the road through two short tunnels and one longer tunnel to the Buffalo Bill Dam on the Shoshoni River built in 1910 (free to see). The dam is in a very scenic location on the river! While we were there, the weather turned colder and ominous—remember, we are on a scooter—and we nearly froze going back to base. That evening, we had a good chuckwagon dinner buffet and western musical entertainment at the Cody Cattle Company.

The next day, after a little maintenance and shopping, we took off on the 120 along the Wind River; the canyons along the river are spectacular! We got on the 20 at Thermopolis (hot springs there); saw the scenic features of Boysen State Park and Boysen State Reservoir; through Shoshoni to Riverton, a large town with all the facilities; had lunch at Taco Bell; and observed many seagulls. (What are they doing there?)

Then it was on to Dubois, Wyoming, the route taking us through some very scenic hills, mountains, buttes, and canyons. By the way, Dubois has a giant jackalope. We stayed the night in a city park.

Next day (Thursday), we headed to Grand Teton National Park. A beautiful drive, and we saw much wildlife—such as elk, deer, and antelope. We arrived in Jackson, had lunch near the visitor center, then drove over to Jackson Hole at the Teton Village. Nice rustic shops and inns cater to the skiers.

We got on the tramway two-and-a-half miles up to the top of Mount Rendezvous—10,400 feet. The view was like no other! You could see the entire Teton range almost at eye level, many lakes, other ranges, many miles of the Snake River. We had hot chocolate at the top café. (They served waffles there for some reason.) The trip up took us over four thousand feet up in elevation—rough climbing stairs! And yes, it was pretty cold up there.

After coming back down, we figured we had already seen the Tetons; no need to go into the park. So we left, heading south on the 26, 89, 189, 191 (they have a lot of numbers) through yet more river rapid areas and canyons. We got a free freshwater fill-up at an RV park then drove a little more before stopping for the night at a roadside info/pullout area close to Pinedale. Not every day you get to play in the snow in late *June!*

Fourth of July, 2010

Happy Fourth, everyone!

From Pinedale rest stop we proceeded to Rock Springs, Wyoming, and stayed there overnight. Our coach battery was still giving us problems, so I worked on the connections extensively. I think I got it back to normal, although the battery was damaged and won't hold a charge quite like it did.

Then after researching RV parks in and around Cheyenne, we found only two parks with spaces left; Cheyenne Frontier Days has all the hotels, RV parks, and campgrounds all booked up in July. We decided to drive to Cheyenne to rent a future spot while we could. Joe's Restaurant, Bar, and RV Park isn't much to look at but had a space for $280 a month plus electric, and the folks were nice. From there we drove a few miles to the Wyoming welcome center I-25 at I-80 to stay the night; free Wi-Fi!

With a few days left in June, we decided to see some sights in east central Wyoming, so we took off on the I-25 northward to Casper. The next day, we left the chamber of commerce/info center (where we parked overnight in the back of the facility) a few miles up the road to the Fort Caspar Museum, where they had log buildings and an informative walking tour.

Then we headed down the 220 about fifty miles to Independence Rock State Historical site—a huge rock dome which the 1800s pioneers stopped at and used for a point of reference; many of these people signed their names on the rock face. We saw a rattler in a crack on the rock and hightailed it away from there.

From there we drove a few miles to see the Devil's Gate, simply a gap in the hills also used as a reference point. After leaving the "gate," we went back to Casper and stayed the night at—you guessed it—Walmart.

Next day (Tuesday), we headed south to Glenrock and visited the Dinosaur Museum—a very cool and informative venue that even offers the excitement of going on a "dig" with the scientists (we didn't go; no dig this day). Next we had lunch and Wi-Fi at McDonald's in Douglas, then went east on U.S. 26 to the Register Cliffs site, where pioneers (and others) wrote their names during their travels on the Oregon—Mormon—California Trail.

Then one mile over to the Oregon Trail Ruts, actual tracks carved into the rocky countryside by the thousands of wagons passing through—very impressive. From there we continued on to Fort Laramie, perhaps the most important outpost on the westward trail. The site has many buildings—original and restored—from the 1830s on, plus items and artifacts used by the workers and soldiers. From there we drove several miles back to a highway rest area where we stayed the night.

Oh, I left out the Ayers Natural Bridge between Glenrock and Douglas—an awesome rock-bridge formation over the North Platte River. There is a nice park and camping facilities there at the natural bridge, as well as outstanding red canyon views.

The next day, we drove down to Cheyenne and set up camp at T Joe's RV Park. There is a firework stand in the same (large) parking lot, so we should expect some explosions during the days leading up to the Fourth of July.

July 5, 2010

We haven't been doing much since we got here in Cheyenne, but today we rode the Honda into downtown. We took a ninety-minute city tour that included twenty-plus minutes in the Old West Museum on the Cheyenne Frontier Days grounds. We had lunch at Sanfords—good food and tons of nostalgic decor and crazy artifacts (old bicycles, hubcaps, championship banners, Elvis statue, etc.)

Then we took a thirty-minute horse-drawn carriage ride through downtown, basically repeating most of the trolley tour.

Later we went back to the CFD grounds and bought tickets to the Professional Bull Riders' performance on July 27 and Clay Walker on July 28.

One thing about the weather here: it's mostly dry (although it can rain every afternoon), mild days, cool nights subject to change on a moment's notice.

We will be preparing to make a trip into next week into Colorado.

July 11, 2010

After waiting for mail that never came, we hit the I-25 Saturday afternoon southbound toward Fort Collins. We then got on the 14 but lost it, got directions, and successfully headed west toward Steamboat Springs. Highway 14 goes through the Poudre River canyon—a twisting, turning, winding, gnarly road with great views of river rapids, waterfalls, mountains, and canyon walls.

After fueling up in Walden, we decided to continue (it was 7:00 p.m.) an hour and a half into Steamboat Springs. Upon arriving, we parked for the night at public lot set up for the balloon rodeo the next day!

We got up at 5:30 a.m. after little or no sleep and boarded a bus to the rodeo. It was a really neat event; we saw the whole balloon process from start to finish! There were about forty hot-air balloons doing tasks of dipping the balloon basket into the nearby lake; dropping beanbags onto targets; and, of course, ascending and descending properly.

After the balloon rodeo, we got on the U.S. 40 headed to Denver—nice mountain views. On the way, we found the Buffalo Bill Grave and Museum which was an adventure getting to, as the facility is on top of a huge hill—a very steep climb for a motorhome. Besides the cool museum, there is a spectacular view of Denver and seemingly hundreds of miles of landscape from the observation decks.

Upon leaving the B. B. Museum, we got back on the interstate and used McDonald's Wi-Fi to find a campground (Walmart) close to Denver where we stayed the night.

July 14, 2010

Greetings from Colorado!

So far we haven't been disappointed in this beautiful state! So after a quasi we're-lost trip through downtown Denver (we wanted to see Coors Field and Mile High Stadium), we got on the I-25 south toward Colorado Springs.

Upon arrival, we drove through the Garden of the Gods—a red rock geological spectacle which has a lot of rocks, boulders, and other features which the public can hike, bike, climb, photograph, etc. While driving through, our brakes were trying to overheat and not wanting to stop our rig.

After lunch, we drove on to Manitou Springs and had difficulty finding parking, but the attendants hooked us up close to the train depot to Pikes Peak! We bought the first tickets available, so we had to wait 'til 4:00 p.m. for the train. The long, slow ride up the mountains was nothing short of breathtaking (literally; it's difficult breathing up there). We saw some waterfalls, old structures, wildlife (marmots and ravens), killer view of the lakes, forest, plains, mountains, and tiny towns below.

At the summit (14,105 feet. Ouch!), we got off the train and walked around what seemed to be the top of the earth or a view from near-earth orbit! The air is really thin up there, and we were feeling woozy—not sick, but just loopy. On the trip down, we passed the time by talking to a nice couple from Texas.

Later that evening, after almost hitting a stupid motorcyclist, we had dinner at Rudy's BBQ then tried to park for the night at Walmart, but security ran us off (first time that's happened); so we went next door to park alongside the Office Depot.

Tuesday, we got on the 24 west to Canon City (pronounced *canyon*), then over to Royal Gorge Park. We thought we'd have to choose which activities to do (or could afford), but it turns out they have a day pass for only $25 which includes all but the crazy bungee thing and horseback ride. The Gorge is a magnificent marvel of nature, and the bridge gives a great view at a thousand feet over the Arkansas River!

We rode the Incline Railway (1,200 feet) almost straight down to the river's edge; we saw many kayakers and rafters, one of which spilled two passengers including the guide (but got back on). On the other side of the gorge, we got on the aerial tramway which carries about twenty people over two thousand feet across without supports (other than the cable).

We also walked across the bridge, rode the two-horse-drawn carriage, saw a gunfight in the street of the old west town, saw wildlife aboard the trolley (elk; mountain sheep; burros; buffalo, including one white). Before leaving, we got on the little train that goes in a short loop that has fake sights of Yellowstone, Boot Hill, Box Canyon, Rattlesnake Gulch, etc. All in all one of the best places we've ever spent a day at!

From the Royal Gorge, we got on the 9 (only paved road to Cripple Creek from here, but it turned out to have some dirt portions) and drove seemingly forever before getting to Cripple Creek. In town, we found a dirt bus lot to park in; we were able to pirate some nearby electricity off the engine heater power sockets.

Forgot to mention, last night I was trying to open a can of biscuits. After pounding on it maybe ten times, it finally popped (exploded) *all over* the RV in about an eight-foot radial pattern. I salvaged most of the biscuits. (It's just sprinkles!)

Wednesday morning, a coyote walked up close by, and Sue got pics. We travelled the 5: a half mile over to Victor to go into the gold mine via a giant truck; however, we couldn't get tickets (capacity of fourteen) and didn't want to wait six hours for the next tour. So we toured the mining museum and panned for gold in their little horse trough, a lot of iron pyrite (fool's gold) and a few small gemstones but little or no gold of any significance. Disappointed, we left Victor on the 67, back through Manitou Springs to Colorado Springs, onto the interstate, back to Cheyenne (our temporary "home").

July 15–31, 2010

Hello, y'all.

We are winding up our stay in Cheyenne, Wyoming, and today (Saturday) we have a ton of chores to accomplish as we will be leaving Wyoming tomorrow. As this is a small town for a capital city, we now know this town like the back of our hand. We have had a lot of downtime anticipating the start of Cheyenne Frontier Days, but the event was worth the wait! I will condense down the timeline of events during CFD, hitting the highlights:

July 17: Saw *Despicable Me* in 3D at the Frontier Mall; it was just okay.

July 18: Watched the Cheyenne Frontier Days cattle drive (550 head, really neat) then took off on a scenic ride on Wyoming highway 34, between Chugwater and Laramie. We stopped at a rest area that contained a large Lincoln memorial statue then just avoided a wicked rainstorm on the way "home."

July 20: Sheila, the lady next door, cooked us buffalo burgers. Then later, a guy named Steve helped me replace a rather noisy universal joint on the motor home.

July 21: Went online and purchased a seven-day Alaska cruise on Royal Caribbean's Rhapsody of the Seas from Seattle to Juneau and back on August 20–27.

July 23: Went to the mall, saw *Inception* movie; we liked it.

July 24: Went downtown for the CFD parade; it was lengthy but interesting. We drove close to the Frontier Park and parked in the neighborhood. So-so grand entrance (the horsemen were a little rusty), but nice rodeo: three sessions of bull riding, calf roping, steer wrestling, bareback bronc riding, team roping, saddle bronc riding, colt-to-mare race, wild horse race (crazy!), girl trick riders, and barrel racing.

Afterward, we got in the placement line for standing-room-only tickets for Brooks & Dunn; despite standing up from about 5:00 p.m. 'til the show was over (around 11:00 p.m.), it was a killer show! By the way, this is their last concert tour.

July 25: went to Frontier Park and saw the Aaron Tippin/Neal McCoy concert. Tippin was really good, but McCoy was okay. Late that night, I spoke to my longtime friend Dan Austin in Oregon; we will be in his town in August.

July 26: went to the CFD rodeo, left the grounds for dinner (much cheaper at Wendy's), came back for the Professional Bull Riders' night show. We saw Chris Shivers, Dusty LaBeth, Shane Proctor, Sean Willingham, and others. Forty bull riders compete, then the top ten go in the finals. With Sue and I being big PBR fans, this had been something we've always wanted to attend; we had a blast!

July 27: CFD rodeo event, came home, left again, and had dinner at Taco Johns. Then on to the PBR day two event. We saw Tony Mendes, Cord McCoy, Brandon Clark, and Wiley Peterson to name a few. Lots of bulls ridden tonight! Good close-up fireworks show afterward!

July 28: been enjoying good weather lately. We drove over to the Laramie County Community College and watched the thirty-minute Thunderbirds airshow, then on to downtown for the street gunfight/show.

From there we went to Chilis for lunch, then over to Sierra Trading Post for free T-shirts. Later on, it was back to CFD grounds for the Clay Walker concert. Opening act Glen Templeton was okay, but Clay Walker was great!

July 30: drove downtown for the big pancake breakfast (ten thousand to twelve thousand estimated people) and enjoyed the food and entertainment. Next, around the corner to the Cowgirl Museum then back to Sierra Trading Post for more free T-shirts. (They have coupons on a lot of ticket stubs, magazines, brochures, etc.) And next, to the CFD rodeo—our last CFD entertainment.

Afterward, we went to Walmart to load up on groceries. We got carried away buying but managed to get all the stuff onto the Honda somehow. (It looked like the truck on the Beverly Hillbillies, I think.)

July 31: just so you know what needs to happen before we head back out on the road:

- Wash three loads of clothes.
- Put up the TV, VCR, helmets, shoes, books, video game unit, vests, jackets, dishes, remotes, converter box, and anything else not bolted down.
- Fill the shower with clothes boxes.
- Clean the house.
- Drain the black-and-gray water tanks.
- Unhook the sewer hose and stow it.
- Unhook the power cord and stow it.
- Filter water and fill jugs.
- Fill up the freshwater tank.
- Put up the spare propane tank and stove.
- Put the Honda and scooter onto the trailer to strap down.
- Lock up the generator and gas cans.
- Meet with manager to settle the electric bill.
- Fuel up the motor home and gas cans.
- Check fluids and batteries and tire pressures.
- Hook up trailer to the motor home.
- Make sure nothing is left behind.

From Cheyenne, we will travel into Colorado, seeing some sights along the I-70 as we go west into Utah, Idaho, and Oregon.

Hope everyone is having a safe and enjoyable summer!

Greetings from the Austin residence in La Grande, Oregon!

After having to cut off the stem of our bulldog jack we left Cheyenne heading south on the I-25. Having a little brake difficulty, we stopped for the night in Walmart's lot in Denver.

The next day (Monday), we headed west on the feared stretch of I-70, toward Grand Junction. Nice trip through the Rockies—lots of high elevations, beautiful mountain scenery, and great view of Dillon Reservoir and mountains alongside Frisco, Colorado. Many ski towns on this route.

We passed through Glenwood Canyon then stopped at Glenwood Springs, where we bussed up (*way* up) a mountain to see Glenwood Caverns and the village—decent cavern/tour and a nice view way up there. The village is actually a tourist Mecca with Alpine sled, tramway, arcade, thrill ride, and gift shops. We decided not to do the Springs: too many people, not a hundred percent authentic, and too much money. Side note: our fuel gauge worked today (1st time).

Next morning, we hit the road headed toward Utah; not much to look at once you clear the mountains and hills. However, along the way, we did find Rifle Falls State Park, eighty-foot waterfalls with many trails and scenic vantage points. From there we drove on into Utah, stopping for the night at the welcome center.

Wednesday morning took us to Moab, Utah, via the U.S. 191. We rented an RV space for two days then took off on the Honda to Arches National Park. We bought the year pass for $80 then drove through the magnificent arches, spires, red rock mesas, canyons, and valleys of many colors. Despite the nearby threat of rain, we hung on to see all of this spectacular natural wonder.

The next day, despite the threat of rain/thunder, we set out on the Honda toward the Canyonlands National Park. It was a decent ride to the entrance; however, most of the features are hidden until you get really close. The canyons, buttes, and other formations are nearly as good as the Grand Canyon! There are many viewing points and some trails to take.

After leaving the park, we refueled, shed our jackets, then headed south of Moab to the Needles Overlook and the Anticline Overlook. It was twenty-two miles up and down a narrow-paved road with many cattle bridges. This vantage point of the Canyonlands shows the north, south, and west sides of the canyons. We saw the needles, the north and south pistol spires, many buttes, mesas, the Green River, and Colorado River.

On the way home, we got very close to a thunderstorm which displayed a nice rainbow. Along the way, we viewed the Wilson Arch, which is right alongside the highway.

Friday, we prepared to leave the Moab Rim RV Park then set out northward on U.S. 191, then I-70, then U.S. 6 toward Salt Lake City. We stopped in Price, Utah, and visited the Prehistoric Museum (Utah State University Eastern). They have a lot of dinosaur bones, fossils, and skeletons; also fossils of plants, trees, and various crustaceans; also ancient Indian artifacts.

We left that facility and traveled to the I-15, where we stopped for the night at (not again!) Walmart near Orem. Saturday, we got back on the interstate then quickly exited onto Highway 92 toward the Timpanogos Cave. We found the park but had trouble finding parking for our forty-nine-foot train. We tried to get on the tour for the cave but would've had to wait many hours, so we settled for a virtual tour on their computer (I know, I know!).

We then left the park, headed to Kennecott Copper Mine. After receiving some poor directions plus a steep climb, we arrived at the mine. The mine and all the facilities are *huge!* The open pit—the world's largest—is two-and-a-half miles across and 3/4-miles deep. They use earth-moving vehicles as large as a house.

Inside the visitor center, we watched an impressive video about the company and the entire operation then toured the info kiosks. Leaving the mine, we got back on I-15 to Loop 215 to I-80 to Highway 65, which turned out to be a long route through the mountains. We were hoping to get to I-84 to find the Devil's Slide, but we wound up pulling over on the side of the highway for the night due to overheated brakes.

After testing the brakes, we set out to find the Devil's Slide; no problem, it's right on the interstate. Cool rock formation: it almost looks manmade. Next we got back on the I-15 via the U.S. 89 to try to see the Great Salt Lake and Salt Lake City. No luck on the lake, but the Interstates 215, 80, 15 go right through downtown.

Next we drove north to the highway 13 near Brigham City and followed the signs to the Golden Spike Monument near Promontory, Utah. Nice exhibits, monument, steam-engine locomotive demonstration and narrative.

From the spike, we headed north into Idaho. After stopping for fuel in Pocatello, we made it to Idaho Falls, parked at Camp Walmart, and walked over to Famous Dave's BBQ for supper. By the way, we did catch some glimpses of the Great Salt Lake from various points along the I-15.

Good day, mates! (Where'd that come from?)

This morning we walked a few blocks to see the Idaho Falls. The falls were nice and extended way up the Snake River but was flanked by an unsightly spillway. Next we set out west on the U.S. 20 toward the Craters of the Moon National Monument. Basically this region (which actually covers much of southern Idaho) was covered by flowing and spewing lava thousands of years ago. We drove through, stopping and hiking to see some formations, hills, caves, and plant life. Oh yeah, before arriving at the Craters of the Moon National Monument and Preserve, we stopped to see the EBR-1 nuclear power plant; the first of its kind! Not only did we go onto the property, but they let folks go deep into the entire facility! No, not any residual radiation there, but extremely interesting stuff.

After Craters, we stopped for fuel in Carey when I noticed the trailer hitch was sagging considerably and the framework was separating. After emergency chain-up, we continued into Twin Falls, Idaho on highway 93, staying the night at an empty lot in town.

The next morning, when we tried to leave, the motor home wouldn't start. Yikes! Many hours later, I called for a wrecker to tow us down the road to the mechanic. (He wouldn't drive a few blocks to us.) He diagnosed the faulty ignition module and replaced it, then we're hooked to the trailer and were on our way again.

Before leaving the town, we decided to go ahead and see the falls. The hard-to-get-to location was well worth the hassle as the Shoshoni Falls are beautiful and picturesque. From there, we took off west down the I-84 toward Boise, stopping for the night at a rest area.

This morning, we continued west on the I-84, stopping for fuel in Boise, before heading finally into La Grande, Oregon, where we got directions from Dan to the local Laundromat. From there, Katherine escorted us to their house. Later that evening, we all went to the Flying J restaurant, then home to finish hookups (on the motor home, you dirty-minded people) and to start catching up on the last twenty to twenty-five years.

Thursday, we went into town for some supplies, fuel, and propane and also to the NAPA auto parts for several maintenance and repair items: oil, filter, brake and tranny fluid, spark plug wires, coolant. That evening, we all went to KFC's buffet (first time for me), and afterward, they drove us way up a hill/mountain to see Morgan's Lake (looks like a good fishin' hole) then home for the night.

The next few days were spent doing some maintenance and minor repairs, such as the broken bathroom vent cover. Also during that time, we all went to Bud Jackson's Sportsman Bar and Grill to shoot pool, and Dan and I did some cutting/welding on our bumper, frame, and bulldog jack. Then we installed the spare (wheeled) jack that I'd been carrying the entire trip.

On Sunday Dan, Sue, Nick (one of the sons), and I set out to Lake Wallowa, Oregon. Dan was a great tour guide along the way, and he stopped at the Wallowa River where he showed us how to fly-fish. (He quickly caught two trout.) Then it was over to a favorite campground higher up in the mountains, alongside a nice cascading stream.

Then we drove through some small towns and slowly through Joseph (Chief Joseph)—a nice little historic town—before arriving at the lake. We fished later on with worms, with no luck; no bites at all. No matter, the scenery is beautiful there.

From there we headed home for the night, where Sue and I managed to catch up on some episodes of Big Brother (bummer—no decent broadcast TV in La Grande except for PBS stations) on the computer via some pirated Wi-Fi that mysteriously exists in their neighborhood (or their house).

Monday through Thursday was spent mostly around the house—playing Tetris and Hotshots Golf on the PlayStation2; visiting and playing dominoes with Dan and Katherine; working on the gray tank's plumbing (the work on an RV is never-ending); putting the finishing touches on the weld work; going out to dinner a few times; surfing the worldwide web; and, best of all, packing and preparing everything for our Alaskan cruise coming up tomorrow, Friday, the 20th of August.

Hi again. At 5:00 a.m. this fine Friday morning, we got up, packed our luggage onto Dan's old pickup, and headed west on the I-84 then the I-82 to the I-90 westbound, arriving in a Seattle suburb close to 12:00 p.m. Along the way, we saw many vineyards, apple and peach orchards, nice canyons, a cheese factory (I'd like to have had the time to tour it), lakes, and mountains. Included were Mount Hood and Mount Rainier. We parked the truck and took a cab to the Pier 91 terminal. We got some excellent pics along the way, including the famous fish market and the Space Needle. We got onto the ship without a hitch; that evening, we saw a *Welcome Aboard* show, which included a stand-up comic.

The next day, Saturday was mostly spent wandering around the boat; it was kind of cold outside, especially when the sun was hidden. We saw some informative seminars, toured some shops, ate a lot, and watched *Leap Year* (chick flick, yuck) that afternoon.

During a trip outside, we saw a whale spray off in the distance. After supper at the buffet, we watched the comedian/musician Gary Mule Deer perform in the big theater—good show!

Sunday was cool and rainy, which is typical for the northern west coast, I hear. After breakfast, we exited the ship in Juneau, Alaska, and went to the tour waiting area—or so we thought. We almost missed our bus, as we were in the wrong place. The short, quick ride through Juneau left us wanting more; the guide seemed to be in a big hurry. The exploration of Mendenhall Glacier, though, was really neat; we never saw anything like it!

After our hour was up, we went back into town where Sue and I got off the bus and explored Juneau on our own, mostly looking for souvenirs. One notable building was a visitor info center whose front was composed entirely of nine thousand pieces of driftwood.

Later that evening, back on the ship, we saw the *Piano Man* show in the theater performed by the ship's song/dance group. Good show.

Monday, the ship docked in Skagway, Alaska, and after an early breakfast, we left the ship to tour the town and White Pass. This tour was nice and informative. We toured the old graveyard, saw magnificent scenery, and many waterfalls.

After crossing into Canada and stopping at the shortest suspension bridge in North America in the Torment Valley, we headed back to Skagway. We got off the bus in downtown, going through many shops, saloons, and tour brokers. The Klondike Gold Rush Museum was interesting and showed a cool video of those gold rush days.

While going back to the ship, we spotted two seals in the harbor (or one seal in two places); we weren't quick enough for pics. That evening, we filled out a few postcards; and after dinner, we saw the country/western show at the theater. Today we are farther north latitude than we have ever been. If it weren't cloudy at night, we might've seen the northern lights.

Overnight, we sailed to the Tracy Arm Fjord—a narrow strait leading to the Sawyer Glacier. The weather is great this morning! The Rhapsody of the Seas stopped within a half mile of the glacier then spun slowly 180 degrees. This was, for me, the best scenery I've ever seen! Hundreds of waterfalls, snow-capped mountains, and icebergs of many shapes and sizes.

We sighted some whale fins, spouts, and tails. Far in the distance, I saw a rather large whale emerge and splash down spectacularly like that one on the insurance commercial! In a few hours, the weather turned cooler and foggy, and the seas got rougher; so no more whale sightings. That evening, we attended the Motown show by a group called Spectrum (Temptations, Platters, etc.) Good show.

Wednesday was spent at sea. The weather was pretty decent: sunny but chilly. We walked around a lot, played some games at the casino, and watched some of the Little League World Series (a team from Pearland, Texas, was still in it). That evening, we had our first dinner at the Edelweiss Restaurant. We had crab and scallop appetizers then tried the butterfish; it was just so-so. Tonight's show was the ballroom dancing song and dance; it was pretty good.

We went ashore on Thursday in Victoria, British Columbia, Canada, where we took a bus tour of the city. During the tour, we stopped at Craigdarroch Castle, 105 years young. Going through the castle involved climbing five floors' worth of stairs (no elevator). There was a lot of original artifacts, decorations, and personal items. The upper floors gave a nice view of Victoria in many directions.

Next we wound up the tour then walked around downtown where we bought a sandwich at a 7-Eleven store. After that, we started making our way back to the ship, seeing Chinatown and much of the harbor, as well as the Empress Hotel (one can have afternoon tea for a little over a hundred bucks).

Back on the ship, after stuffing ourselves yet again (that darned buffet), we watched the evening show—the *Farewell Show*—which featured a comedy juggler dude.

Early the next morning, they made us get off their ship, so we packed up and went back onto the mainland in Seattle and got back to Dan's old truck for the ride back.

Sue and I headed south on the I-5 toward Portland, but instead of going through town, we decided to go around Portland via the I-205 to pick up the I-84 east of the city. After fueling up, we were headed down the 205 when we saw signs for the Columbia Gorge. We quickly exited to highway 14 and proceeded through the river gorge area; however, we couldn't see much from this side of the river—too many trees.

Well, this twisting, turning, up-and-down road seemed to go on forever. Seeing a sign that said "JCT interstate 82—138 miles," we decided to find a place to cross the river (rather than get lost somewhere in Washington), and soon we lucked upon a $1.00 toll bridge at Hood River (town). We had lunch at Taco Bell (a familiar setting) then got on the I-84 toward La Grande, stopping to look at a huge dam—the Dalles Dam—as well as good views of the gorge. A welcome bonus was the delicious grilled steak and chicken dinner Dan and Katherine fixed for us that evening.

On Sunday, it was nice out, so we got on the Honda for a joyride. First we stopped at the nearby rest stop for maps and Oregon Trail info, then went onto the 203 toward Union, Oregon. This old town (1862) has a historic hotel, school, and many old houses. On the way back, we stopped to see Hot Lake with its 203-degree water and steam coming off it.

The next several days were spent surfing the web (with much difficulty; weak pirated Wi-Fi signal), working on an extension to Dan's workshop, playing video games, watching DVDs, playing cards and dominoes with the Austins, doing laundry, and going out for dinner at a local Mexican restaurant.

On Friday, the third of September, we went to the town of Elgin where Dan works as a machinist at the Boise Sawmill. Risking life, limb, and his job, Dan led us on a grand tour of the facility. The tour took us through the processes whereby a log is turned into a two-by-four board. The second half of the tour took us through the plywood-making facility, the highlight being a killer machine that takes a log and shaves a thin layer around and around the log 'til there's nothing left but a core not much larger than a broomstick! Seeing what all is involved in the lumber making process, it's easy to see why prices are so high for wood.

The next morning, we all got up at the buttcrack of dawn and took off down highway 82 to the first of many stops along the Wallowa River for a day-long fly-fishing adventure. Sue and I both quickly caught our first trout using a fly reel, then we moved on to another spot up the river. No one warned us about the treacherous walking conditions along the bank; we got a real workout.

At one point, the rod separated into two halves, one half trying to escape downstream! Well, I tracked the pole down as it snagged on some rocks; it was quite a chase for a few minutes! A little later, our spot required us (only Dan and me at this point) to wade across a small fast-moving stream to get to the river. Where I went across, there were several large bulls waiting to greet me—one in particular was giving me the evil eye.

I survived that encounter, and with daylight waning and not much luck (except for Dan), we headed back toward La Grande where we stopped for dinner at a Chinese buffet.

Sunday was spent shooting pool with Dan at Bud Jackson's Sportsman Bar and Grill, where I experienced my first order of dry nachos (I wouldn't recommend them even while drinking beer). Monday was a day for last-day visiting with the Austins, washing the RV, and other preparations for leaving tomorrow. Looks like we will be heading back to the Boise area on our way to southern Utah.

Our heartfelt thanks go out to Dan and Katherine for their fellowship and supreme hospitality!

Greetings from Kanab, Utah! (Details to follow; stay tuned.)

After final preparations were executed, we took off eastbound on the I-84 toward Boise, Idaho. The motor home was running increasingly rough along the way, and when we stopped at a rest area upon inspection, I noticed a few of the spark plug wires which I installed had popped off; I guess I didn't mash them on hard enough.

We got back on the highway, and later—when we exited to get fuel—we ran out of gas while waiting for the light to change at the end of the exit ramp (running on five of eight cylinders will burn some extra gas). Luckily, we carry many gas cans, so I only had to endure the embarrassment of refueling there in traffic! Well, we survived that and parked for the night in a vacant lot close to the gas station.

The next morning, we drove over to the Peregrine Fund's World Center for Birds of Prey facility. There are hawks, falcons, eagles, owls, kestrels, kites, and condors live in cages. They have a wealth of information on raptors and falconry. A lady showed us a turkey vulture (buzzard, to you uneducated heathens) up close and personal; and later, a different lady displayed a Peregrine falcon. I highly recommend a visit to this wonderful facility.

Afterward, we drove (in the cold and in the rain) to the Garden of Eden Truck Plaza in Eden, Idaho. The next day, we ate up a lot of miles, winding up just south of Salt Lake City—still cold, windy, and raining. There we found a Sam's Club parking lot and stayed for the night. We have enjoyed being able to watch broadcast TV the last couple of days (we are TV junkies).

The next day, we took off south down the I-15 to Scipio, then east on U.S. 50, to highway 24 where we stopped in Richfield, Utah, for lunch and supplies at Walmart. While parked there, I tightened two squealing belts without busting my knuckles.

From there we got on the 119 all the way to Torrey at the gateway to Capitol Reef National Park. We stayed the night in a vacant lot next to a burger joint.

It was very cold and windy last night (same cold front we've been running from for a few days) but clear and calm this morning. We drove into Capitol Reef National Park, toured the visitor center, then drove the ten-mile scenic road which ended at the Capitol Gorge (the road became dirt and narrower, so we couldn't drive it).

We walked about a quarter mile for many photos then drove the rest of the park on (paved) highway 24. This beautiful and interesting stretch has many colorful monuments and canyons, as well as the old Fruita schoolhouse, fruit orchards, the Capitol Dome formation, and the Fremont Indian Petroglyphs.

We left the park and got on highway 12 toward Bryce Canyon National Park, passing through the Grand Staircase—Escalante Monument (one of the best-kept secrets in America). Highway 12 in this area is a twisting, turning, up-and-down adventure but has many spectacular scenic overlooks! We stopped for the night alongside a rest area in Escalante, Utah.

It was warmer this morning. We went down the 12 to the town of Bryce Canyon (est. 2007) near the entrance to the park. We parked the RV and got on the shuttle bus to hit all the highlights out to Bryce Point. The Bryce Canyon (not really a canyon after all) is chock-full of hoodoos, spires, monuments, and a huge variety of colors and varied landscapes!

After going through the visitor center (including watching a neat video), we went back to the RV to drive the long end of the park eighteen miles to Rainbow Point. Plenty more of the amazing features which abound in this great park, including Thor's Hammer and a huge natural bridge.

After lunch, we got on the 12 to U.S. 89 south toward Kanab. This highway took us through more of the Grand Staircase, Kanab Canyon, and the coral pink sand area. We arrived in Kanab and stopped to visit the Little Hollywood of the West Museum, which has some buildings and artifacts from western movie sets done in the region. This tourist trap did not live up to the hype which preceded it; it was just okay. Afterward we found a vacant lot in town in which to spend the night.

Monday morning, we took off on the Honda, heading south on the ALT 89. The terrain went from flat desert to mountaintops. We stopped at a pullout to view the colorful Vermillion Cliffs. We continued through mostly burned forest and got onto highway 67 south to Grand Canyon National Park, North Rim. We walked out to many viewpoints then had lunch at the deli near the lodge. We left the visitor center and took a road leading to Imperial Point. Best view ever!

At the 8,800 feet elevation, you can see everything well, and the air was clear on this day. We easily viewed features on the other side of the canyon—Marble Canyon, Vermillion Cliffs & mountains 135 miles away. We left the park and headed back to Kanab, staying the night in the same vacant lot in town.

After getting fuel, fresh water, and dumping the black/gray tanks we set out on U.S. 89, then highway 9 toward Zion National Park. This twelve-mile stretch (mostly under vigorous construction at the time) runs through mountains and canyons with many switchbacks; westbound is all downhill and many one-lane stretches. The highway went through an unlit tunnel (one way) over one mile long!

An hour later than we thought we would, we arrived at Zion and, after a bite to eat, boarded the shuttle bus to the first of many stops: The Temple of Sinawava, Weeping Rock, Angels Landing, The Grotto, and Zion Lodge. Zion National Park features huge sandstone monuments/cliffs, some of which are among the largest in the world.

It took two hikes of a mile each—first one along the Virgin River, which created the canyon, and the second to Emerald Pool with its blowing waterfall. After seeing a video in the museum theater, we left the park. Note: Zion was the least scenic park of the "big five" of Utah in our opinion. We then headed south on the 9 and stopped for the night at Walmart (not again!) on the far side of Hurricane, Utah.

Wednesday, we took off south on highway 9 to I-15, south toward Las Vegas, Nevada. After stopping at a Walmart in the city, we decided to find an RV park. We got on the I-515, 93, 95 toward Boulder City and quickly found the $16 per night Roadrunner R. V. Park, where we paid for two nights.

Later we got on the Honda and rode onto The Strip—took many photos of casinos—and the Welcome Sign then headed "home." We thought we were going to die from the heat.

Next morning, we went on the motorcycle down highway 93 through Henderson and Boulder City to Hoover Dam. The facilities and the dam are huge! The tours, parking, and admission to the visitor center are pricey though. The dam is truly a magnificent feat of engineering, and Lake Mead is a beautiful blue. We then came back to the RV park; and later in the evening, we went back to The Strip (Las Vegas Boulevard) to see it at night. We saw the volcano at the Mirage and the fountains at the Bellagio (a must-see). We walked many miles, took a thousand photos, then went back to the house—pretty late for us.

We left Las Vegas early this morning, heading south on the 93. We crossed over Hoover Dam into Arizona. We stopped for lunch and Wi-Fi at McDonalds in Kingman, Arizona, but due to the remodeling taking place, it had no Wi-Fi. We continued east on the I-40 into Williams (gateway to the Grand Canyon and a nostalgic Route 66 town) where we stopped and parked for the night at a roadside park. That evening, we walked over to Rod's Steakhouse for a nice dinner. Unfortunately, it had no TV or Wi-Fi at this location.

We took off this morning (Saturday) on the Honda headed up the 64 toward Grand Canyon National Park, South Rim. We parked at the visitor center and took the shuttle bus to most of the stops along the rim, including some on Desert View Drive at the eastern end of the park. We had spaghetti lunch (it was surprisingly good) at the cafeteria between stops. We left the park later on, arriving back in Williams at sunset. We have come to realize the $80 annual park pass will easily pay for itself after four or five parks!

The next morning, we attempted to leave Williams but instead were compelled to stop at Bearizona, Arizona's new wildlife park. Although still under construction, they let folks in for half price ($11 each). Very nice large drive-through facility where, after a fifteen-minute burros-in-the-road delay, we proceeded through to view buffalo, bobcats, bighorn sheep, *black bears*, gray foxes, and wolves. They also have pens with young bears, bobcats, and the foxes.

Afterward, we took off eastbound to Flagstaff where we found parking at North Arizona University. We then took off on the bike a few miles east to Walnut Canyon National Monument, a beautiful canyon which houses many Sinagua cliff dwellings. After descending about 250 feet using 240 stairs, we saw the interesting dwellings built into the cliffs and overhangs, then huffed and puffed our way back up to the visitor center (note: national monuments are also on the annual park's pass), then walked over to another pueblo on the grounds. After that, we headed back to where we were parked for the night.

On Monday morning, we left Flagstaff heading north on U.S. 89, stopping at Sunset Crater National Monument, where a volcano spewed ash and lava a thousand years ago. Then on the same loop, we saw the Watashi Ruins, a three-story adobe house built high on a sandstone formation and the pueblo village with its many rooms, a ball court, and a "blowhole" which, at this time of year, blows out cool subterranean air!

Next we got back on the 89 to the Navajo National Monument headquarters close to Utah border. The Tsegi Canyon houses a historic Ranger Station and the Betatakin Ruins—a large pueblo community built into a huge arch/cave featured on one wall of the canyon. It was a mile walk over to the viewpoint; while we were gone, the visitor facility closed on us. So we left from there and continued on the 89 to Kayenta, Arizona, where we parked near the McDonald's parking lot. Many homeless(?) Indians (most native Americans don't mind being called Indians!) accosted us at that location, asking for food or money. Later we had Chinese fast-food and called it a night. Fortunately, a guard of some sort ran off the locals.

Next day, we got on the U.S. 163, heading north toward Monument Valley. Many large monuments, buttes, and spires along the way. We stopped at the Navajo Monument Valley visitor center (US parks pass not accepted) after turning down sixty-five-dollar (each) tickets for a pickup truck tour—to features we could clearly see where we were standing! The view was good at the headquarters, and there was a lot of info and artifacts.

After the walkthrough, we exited the park, driving through magnificent scenery on the way to highway 191, which runs south toward the I-40. We stopped at the Canyon de Chelly National Monument with its many overlooks and views of Anasazi pueblo villages from seven hundred to nine hundred years ago. Nice visitor center. From there we continued south to Ganado, where we stopped alongside a gas station for the night.

It rained all night and all day Wednesday, but we plowed on to the 40 then went east to Gallup, New Mexico. We bought two used tires (front end ate up my new tires) then drove to Walmart for supplies. We had dinner at Golden Corral before going back to Walmart to park for the evening.

Thursday, we got on the business I-40/Route 66 then headed south on highway 602 to highway 53, east to El Morro National Monument. We did a half mile hike up the steep steps and walkway to an ancient pueblo ruin and another half mile over to the mountainside, where over two thousand people have left their names and/or messages dating back to Don Juan, 1605!

Also, a runoff pool which provided the only freshwater for miles and miles. We had lunch then drove a few miles down the road to the Bandera Volcano (one of over twenty volcano cones in the region) which last erupted about ten thousand years ago. We hiked up the side of the cone and looked into the cool crater. Also on the property are many collapsed lava tubes, one of which formed a large cave which has ice in it all year round! This privately-owned property is part of the El Malpais National Monument, a scenic volcanic area of the state. From there we hit the I-40 at Grants, New Mexico, staying in a vacant lot (or so we thought) next to train tracks.

After hearing many trains racing back-and-forth—blaring their horns relentlessly through the night—we awoke and hit the road running, arriving later at the Dancing Eagle Casino/RV Park to take advantage of a cheap rate we had heard of. But with no one there to take our money, we instead hooked up to electric and water for a few hours, taking a shower, dumping the tanks, and getting some AC before taking off again.

Our intention was to get to Albuquerque and wait for the balloon fiesta; since we were early, we would find somewhere to go to kill some time. Since we couldn't find a place to park off the 40, we got on the I-25 south and drove to Los Lunas, where we parked for the night at the Walmart.

On Saturday, we continued southbound on the I-25 to the U.S. 60 west in Socorro, over to the Very Large Array radio telescope. What else can I say? Huge! Twenty-seven units, occasionally all moving in unison as directed by someone in a control center—a nice informative visitor center—and a killer video too. We left that facility and headed back to Socorro, got on the U.S. 380 eastbound, passing through the lava beds of the Valley of Fires recreation area. That evening, we stopped at a vacant lot in Carrizozo, New Mexico, to park. No television signal (been happenin' a lot lately), so we had to watch DVDs.

The next day, we continued east a few miles to the town of Capitan, where they have a great museum and a tribute to Smokey Bear (born near there, buried there)—nostalgic artifacts, videos, nice garden, and even the gravesite.

After doing laundry (right next door), it was off to Lincoln, where they have the Lincoln (town) State Monument, many buildings, and an adobe fort from the 1800s. From there we picked up the 70 to Roswell, New Mexico, then south on U.S. 285 to Carlsbad. We stayed the night in a vacant lot on the main drag.

Monday morning, we headed south on the Honda to highway 7 to Carlsbad Caverns National Park. We took a self-guided tour of the Big Room (really huge; the size of fourteen football fields). The elevator taking you down seems to go on forever. After having lunch in the café, we left the park and went back to Carlsbad, packed up, and drove north to Roswell where we stayed the night in a Sear's/Dollar Store parking lot.

The next day, we headed north on the 285 to highway 20—the bumpiest paved road we have encountered on this trip (or any other trip)—to Fort Sumner. We visited the Billy the Kid Museum, memorial, and gravesite; it was very interesting and informative. After lunch, we got on U.S. 84 to Santa Rosa, along I-40 west, then back on 84 northbound to I-25 north to Las Vegas, New Mexico. We stayed overnight in the parking lot beside Comfort Inn.

On Wednesday, we headed south on I-25 to Santa Fe. After an exhaustive but successful search for fuel, we continued into San Felipe Indian Reservation, where we found the San Felipe Casino and its RV park. You can stay for free with no hookups; we lucked into a space with an unlocked electrical panel. Wi-Fi was available on a limited basis. (Note: free pirated Wi-Fi is hard to come by in Utah, Arizona, and New Mexico.)

Thursday, we rode the Honda toward Albuquerque, looking for a closer place to park the RV while in the Albuquerque area. We discovered the Santa Ana Casino in Bernalillo, which just happens to be a park-and-ride location for the balloon fiesta! We came back to San Felipe and packed up, filled up, dumped out, fueled up everything, then drove our train down to Santa Ana Casino where we parked for the evening.

We wound up staying at the casino for the remainder of our time in the Albuquerque area. The next day, we rode the bike into town and saw most of Old Town Albuquerque (I need to establish an abbreviation for Albuquerque!)—many shops with their arts and artisans, some old buildings, an old church, and many tourists milling about.

We stopped for lunch at a nearby Wendy's then rode over to the Balloon Fiesta Visitor Center. We bought tickets for Saturday morning and Thursday evening (includes shuttle bus ride), and after telling the clerk that Thursday is Sue's birthday, he only charged us for one set of tickets!

From there it was over to the Walmart near our casino for groceries and cheap-imitation Albuquerque balloon T-shirts, then back home for the night.

After a three o'clock false-alarm-clock snafu, we got up at 5:30 a.m. then boarded the shuttle bus over to the balloon fiesta. We saw an amazing mass ascension including Darth Vader, cactus, clown, three bumblebees, Smokey the Bear, the Wells Fargo stagecoach, duck, rooster, goofy face, heart, kitty cat (may have been "Felix"), and many others. We came back home after buying a cheap ballcap then went over to the casino for dinner. We had a terrific prime rib dinner then went back home—expect storms tomorrow and gusty winds tonight.

Since we don't take much stock in the crazy weather forecasts in this part of the US, the next day, we left "home" on the Honda bound for Tinkertown, a little east of Albuquerque. After a lunch stop at KFC, we set out on the shortest route around the mountain. Alas, the short-cut road became a dirt road, so we turned around and took the long way: NM 165 to Tramway Boulevard (yes, they have a long cable tramway up to the top of the mountain that overlooks Albuquerque) over to I-40 east to highway 14, north to New Mexico 536.

Tinkertown is a hobby/collection of old nostalgia turned into a museum of sorts. Well worth the effort to get there; some of the old toys and artifacts really take you back to childhood, and they have amazing miniature displays of circuses. We left there and decided (I'll never know why) to stay on 536 to the (dirt) 165—bad idea! It was a very bad, nasty, potholed, rough-winding road that I would hesitate to drive a Jeep on.

Ten white-knuckled miles later, we survived to get back home and watch TV as it began to rain. A little later, we walked to the casino for play cards, which should get us discounts at the buffet.

Monday, we went over to the casino to have a discount lunch buffet with neighboring RV couple Fred and Delores from Wisconsin. After a long chat-filled lunch, Sue and I broke away and spent two-and-a-half hours plus $25 in the casino playing video slots. Later, we went to a nearby McDonald's for drinks and Wi-Fi before retiring for the evening.

Tuesday, we went on the Honda, exploring toward the balloon fiesta grounds; we observed some balloons landing off-site in fields near the road. We looked for and found a motor home for sale—too old, not interested. We continued into Old Town, Albuquerque, and went over to the New Mexico Museum of Natural Science. We toured the facility then watched movies in the Planetarium: one on telescopes and one on stars in the universe—very cool giant panoramic screen and videos! We came home, and later I rode the bicycle over to McDonald's for Wi-Fi then home for the night.

On Wednesday, we didn't do much other than scratching our heads wondering why the batteries weren't charging. Thinking it might be the alternator, I tried to remove it to have it tested, but as fate would have it, you have to take the radiator out to get the long bolt of the alternator out. So I put it all back together and tried some other ideas, leaning toward the many connections that come with having four batteries.

The next day, Sue's birthday, we went over to the casino to play around a while. There wasn't much winning going on, so Sue moved over to the Texas Tea game, playing and winning steadily for over three hours! When time became a concern, we left the casino, went home for lunch, then got on the bus to the balloon fiesta. We saw the chainsaw log-carving event, walked around some exhibits, then sat on the chairs we had brought along, eating corndogs while waiting for the "Glow-deo" to start.

During this down time, we got to meet Mar from the Yahoo RV Basics group, who is travelling south for the winter; it's nice to put a face to the person behind the keyboard. Thanks, Mar, for a nice visit!

Much to our dismay, the event was cancelled due to high winds, but we stayed anyway for the fireworks show due in an hour or so.

The fireworks were surprisingly great, and afterward, we bussed home where we enjoyed Sue's birthday cake. (Note: since the "Glow-deo" was cancelled, our tickets would get us into the Fiesta any other day!)

Sue's pills ran out the next day, and since the online meds haven't arrived yet, we had to call her doctor in Houston for a refill. We then went to McDonald's for Wi-Fi then next door to Wally World to pick up the pills. Later we walked to the casino where Sue once again mastered the same Texas Tea machine, and I didn't master any machines.

Later on, we got on the shuttle to the balloon fiesta using yesterday's tickets. We got our pictures taken at the interesting Texas-on-tour display; used video-enhanced glasses to drive a kayak on a Texas river; and after many killer glowing balloons, fireworks, a ridiculous random chance meetup with my brother, Keith, and sister-in-law, Penny (it's a small world after all), and a good funnel cake, we took the bus back home.

Saturday morning was colder—in the forties—but warmed nicely to the seventies. After a trip to McDonald's for breakfast and Wi-Fi, we went back to Sue's casino (she seems to own it now). Once again, she played the same machine for a long time before finally crapping out; we then had a late lunch/early dinner buffet before going home for the night.

Sunday morning, it was cold—in the forties again. We unhooked the trailer and drove the motor home to Conoco, where we dumped the tanks and filled the freshwater. I discovered the alternator *is* working, just a bad connection somewhere as I had been suspecting.

Later we rode the Honda to McDonald's for Wi-Fi (thank you, McDonald's) then over to Skip and Marlene's (my brother Keith and his wife, Penny's, relatives) house to touch base with them, as we don't have their phone number. Alas, they weren't home, so I wrote a note and left it at their door.

From there we went home for the night. Monday, it was cold again. Another day, another problem with the batteries; I'll get to the bottom of this someday. We went to the post office for info, but of course they were closed because of Columbus Day. Later we went to the casino again to kill some time and eat lunch at the buffet. (It's a wonder we're not three hundred lbs. apiece.) Skip called us in the afternoon to say the package is at the post office, but it is too late today; so we stayed home for the evening.

Tuesday, we packed up our travelling circus and drove through town to the post office. Since the order came in two packages, we only got forty percent of what we ordered on this shipment; the rest would come sometime later.

With time starting to become a factor to our future plans, we decided to leave Albuquerque without the other 60% of the meds. We headed east on the I-40 to Tucumcari, New Mexico, where we ran out of fuel. My astute calculations did us no good as the faulty engineering of the fuel tank and filler tube let us down. We had $300 of mechanic work done basically for nothing (but a lesson learned), plus $135 for a wrecker tow. We stayed the night outside the shop and had dinner across the street at the Pow Wow Restaurant on Route 66.

On Wednesday, after the work was completed on the motor home, we decided to get the right front tire replaced as it was bubbled and shaking. From there we continued east on the I-40 into Amarillo, Texas, where we stayed the night in a Home Depot parking lot.

The next morning, we went on Loop 335 to highway 1541 south to highway 207, then on Park Road 5 into Palo Duro Canyon State Park. We drove through to see the canyon, stopping a couple of times to get out and look. We didn't see the formations we had hoped for; it turns out you have to hike several miles through the canyon to see the good stuff.

We went back to Amarillo and stopped at the Big Texan Steakhouse (because you have to). Cool buildings and decor, but not great food this day. We got back onto the interstate to U.S. 287 south toward Wichita Falls. We arrived at the Walmart off U.S. 281 south of town and were later picked up by my cousins Maggie and Linda.

We met Maggie's husband—Greg—and Cousin Vincent at a local steakhouse. We had a good dinner and visited a long time (not long enough) trying to fill in the gaps of thirty-some-odd years of no contact. Afterward, we were brought back to our RV where we said our goodbyes.

Friday, we left Wichita Falls, heading south on U.S. 281. We arrived in Stephenville, Texas, and contacted Aunt Teeny and Uncle Danny, who picked us up after we found parking refuge at a closed-down Piggly Wiggly.

Later, we all went for a drive through town and stopped for ice cream and Wi-Fi at McDonald's. That evening, we watched the Texas Rangers play versus the New York Yankees, then my uncle took us back to the RV for the night. (They offered for us to stay at their house, but we declined.)

The next morning, we left Stephenville on the U.S. 377 north toward Fort Worth then I-20 east to Dallas. We got on the familiar I-45 to find the Texas State Fair. We found the grounds and, after some circling around, the neighborhood found an old church to park at (for $20; the others wanted $45).

We entered the fairgrounds and saw a dog stunt show, new car exhibits, butterfly garden, Big Tex, and rode the Skyway cable car from one end to the other. We also attended a cookbook writer's demo (she gave us samples, which we carried home) and had to eat some fried butter, which was pretty good. Satisfied, we left the park and drove to the Flying J, I-45 at I-20, to park for the night.

On Sunday, October 17—the last day of our trip—we left Dallas, heading south on I-45 toward Houston. We stopped in Madisonville at McDonald's, but there was no Wi-Fi there. After fueling up (for the last time on this trip) we drove down to the rest area near Huntsville, but it had no good Wi-Fi connection (par for the course). We continued into the Houston area and found parking readily available in a vacant lot behind Discount Tire, behind Almeda Mall. No, not a Walmart.

Epilogue

If you are reading this, then you most likely have purchased this book, for which I am sincerely grateful! Did I plan on taking ten-plus years to get this done? I don't think so. I will put it out there that this was God's plan for me. On January 1, 2021, I woke up with a (sudden) determination to finish the book. I realized that the only thing holding me back was me. Here are some lessons I learned along the way:

- Life happens.
- Take notes.
- Set aside time for yourself.
- Make goals, but outline *how* to achieve them.
- Believe in yourself.
- Ask for help or advice, but don't take it as gospel.
- Don't overstretch yourself or your limitations, but challenge yourself to try harder.
- Keep in touch with friends and family.
- Do things that make you happy.
- Look at other literary works for layouts, formatting, etc.
- Take responsibility for your own actions.
- You won't get the best results when you are tired or busy with other obligations.
- Put your thoughts into words and print the way you see fit, not how others believe you should do it.
- Pray and thank God every day for everything you have and have had.

- Use all the tools the world gives you.
- See things from other people's perspective and give grace.
- Instead of making excuses, make new commitments and plans.
- Take lots of pictures, but not at the expense of the moment.
- Save your pictures in multiple sites and formats.
- Use the gifts that God gave you—and continues to give you—wisely.
- *Stop!* At some point you must accept what you have done as the finished product.

Mom's and stepmother's health continue to improve. My son and his wife are now legal adoptive parents! Legally welcome Ana Ruby to the Patterson family!

My wife has been battling a variety of infections for what seems like months but is getting better.

I have survived another "snow season" in Houston. What, I never got around to telling you what our company does in the cold months? We take cocktail ice and feed it into a machine that pulverizes it into "snow" for folks to play in. Huge business here in the Gulf Coast region.

The rest of the year, I do anything and everything in the company operation including dispatch, delivery, fleet management and maintenance, purchasing, inventory, hiring, training, discipline, and any other tasks associated with ice distribution.

Meanwhile, I'm going to start wearing the gorilla mask since we are required to wear masks in many public places anyway.

I will get serious about the bus project, starting with the floor. During the last several months, we have been accumulating items for the bus: water pump, water and wastewater-holding tanks, 7,000-watt inverter, toilet, vanity, sink, refrigerator, convection oven, and a few other things. I thought that part of this process would be to give up on activities that were counterproductive or—at minimum—a waste of time; but I have concluded that if it makes you happy, then keep doing it! Thus, I still play the online slot games.

I spent the better part of the day piecing together all the emails and other assorted messages into a single body of work. Then I retrieved the blog posts from the 2010 voyage and put them in order. Although this gave me a sense of accomplishment, I knew there was still some work to be done not only on the book work but on the details post-writing. Thank goodness for spell-check and grammar check!

I will need to choose some photos and decide on the placement in the story. I will need to submit the work to a couple of random people for critiquing. I will need to submit the manuscript to the publisher.

I might have rushed sending the manuscript; they sent it back for photos, and in the course of putting photos in the book body, I cleaned up some rough spots.

What is the next chapter of my life? Only God knows. I'm just going to keep plugging away at it one day at a time. Tentative plans are that after we go on our Cancun vacation, I will contact some companies that manufacture RVs, continue to go to work and earn a living, keep chipping away at the bus project, and possibly write a follow-up book.

Almost time for church to begin.

Life goes on. But now life includes this book! (Thank God.)

The end.

About the Author

Robert Allen Patterson Sr. is a part-time author and full-time blue-collar worker at a local ice distributor in Houston, Texas. The youngest of five baby boomer children, he grew up in the Texas Gulf coast area and, to this day, lives in a Houston, Texas, suburb with his wife Paige and three rambunctious cats.